Financial Literacy for Teens

Parents' Guide

Discover How to Teach Teenagers Smart Money Skills to Budget, Save, & Invest for a Secure Future

Raman Keane

Table of Contents

Introduction

Most people I know have made a mistake when it comes to money—some bigger than others. Although, in some cases, it may not have long-term consequences, there are certain mistakes that we will pay for in the years to come. Can you think of one of those bad decisions that changed your life that you may or may not still be recovering from? Or one that may have changed your life entirely if you made a different decision? What if you could influence your teen positively to avoid making these life-altering money mistakes?

Whether it's one big mistake, a bad decision, or multiple small decisions, the outcome will be the same, and it can be avoided if we teach them about money instead of avoiding the subject completely. For some reason, talking about money has become a sensitive and taboo subject in many households globally, and it shows. According to Fay (2023), the combined American household debt at the end of 2022 hit a record $16.9 trillion, and that's just the United States of America.

Being part of this statistic is easier than you might think. I know a few people who have fallen victim to it, including myself. Most of us have had debt at some point in our lives, and it's nothing to be ashamed of. We explore the good and the bad debt in Chapter 3. It's definitely not always a bad thing, but it can be if we're constantly making bad decisions.

Once you've maxed out the limit, it becomes more difficult to manage the minimum payments and still make provision for emergency purchases (if you don't have an emergency fund). The compounding interest makes it nearly impossible to pay a large portion every month if you're already cash-strapped. The solution most people see out of this situation is to get a second credit card or take out a personal loan to keep their heads above water. It's a slippery slope, especially once your debt-to-income ratio becomes too high.

If you're in a similar situation or see yourself (or someone you know) going down that road, you're not alone. The important thing to remember is that it's never too late to get help. With the right guidance, anyone can learn from mistakes and become financially literate. No one should live in constant anxiety over their financial situation. Money should be a tool to help us achieve what we want in life. Not the decision-maker on what we can and can't do.

By equipping your teen now with the right tools, you can help them achieve financial success and avoid common mistakes. Building up a savings account from a young age is pivotal to financial freedom and success. Starting early to cultivate healthy money habits, understanding debt, knowing how to invest, knowing what role insurance plays in safeguarding savings, and planning for early retirement can all contribute to living a financially free life.

A survey by Stockpile, Inc. (2022) revealed that up to 64% of teens rely on their parents to prepare them with the financial knowledge they need. However, only around 20% of parents actually talk about money and money habits in the household. Your teen is relying on you to help them build the financial future they deserve, so it's pivotal that you educate them about finances and help them become financially literate. If you are in the same position and never had those conversations with your parents, you're in the right place. It's never too late to learn.

While all parents have good intentions for their children's future and want to teach them the necessary skills, they may feel lost when it comes to introducing financial topics. Therefore, in this book, we will use the P.R.O.S.P.E.R. approach as our guiding framework:

- **P:** Planning the budget, saving money, and tracking expenses. In Chapter 1, we will focus on the basics. These are so important because, without them, the rest will be difficult to navigate.
- **R:** Recognizing and using the power of compound interest. Compound interest can be complex to understand, but once you do, it's a real game-changer. This is why we have the entire Chapter 2 dedicated to it.
- **O:** Overcoming debt stress. Whether your teen currently has debt or not, this is such an important concept to cover. It could help prevent them from getting into debt. We'll discuss this in Chapter 3.
- **S:** Securing a part-time job and safeguarding your money for emergencies. In Chapters 4 and 5, we explore getting a job and buying different insurance for the *what-ifs*.
- **P:** Planting the seeds of financial success through investing. Chapter 6 is dedicated to investing and how that works. We only cover the basics because it can become quite complex.
- **E:** Eliminating emotional influences from financial decisions. Sometimes, we allow our emotions to control our spending. Peer pressure and being part of the "in crowd" can be important to teens, and in Chapter 7, we will explore how that affects their spending habits and how to support them.
- **R:** Retiring rich by planning and taking action early. It's never too early to start thinking about retirement. The sooner you start, the better. Chapter 8 deals with action steps you can discuss with your teens to help them plan and prepare for retirement.

An excellent example of someone who was taught how to do business and manage their money is Cameron Johnson. From a young age, he began creating greeting cards. This quickly turned into a toolbar service business, and he became a millionaire when he was a high school senior. We can't all compare ourselves to Cameron, but it's an excellent catalyst to get the motivation going.

This book will equip you with the relevant knowledge and tools needed to help your teen get started on this journey, and you might even learn a thing or two.

I have worked hard to achieve financial security, and I am passionate about personal finance and money management. I've seen what financial illiteracy does to individuals and families and how difficult it is to recover once you fall into the black hole. Because of this, I've spent years researching the best ways to reach financial freedom. Everyone has the potential to have financial security and live a good life. The only thing standing in between your teen and the life they've always wanted is knowledge.

Are you ready to enable yourself and your teen to be more financially literate and learn the secrets of financial freedom? Let's get into it.

Chapter 1

Planning the Budget, Saving Money, and Tracking Expenses

"Do not save what is left after spending; instead, spend what is left after saving."
— **Warren Buffet** —

This is probably one of the best pieces of advice and one of the best-kept secrets of wealthy individuals that Warren Buffett could have shared with the world. But we'll get to the actual saving later. What's important in this chapter is what you do with the remainder of your money after you save. Without a proper budget and expense tracking, making ends meet may be challenging regardless of the amount of money you earn.

If we had unlimited money, we would buy everything on a whim. There is no reason to think twice about buying the newest iPhone or Aston Martin, but very few people can do that. Most of us need to allocate money towards our expenses and save for the more expensive nice-to-haves.

A common mistake young adults tend to make once they start earning money is to spend it on whatever their heart desires at the moment without thinking about the rest of the month. Sometimes, the reason they can do that is because their parents will bail them out when they get into trouble. Now, moms and dads, I know we mean well, but it's time they learn how to budget and manage their money efficiently, or else you'll be supporting them for the rest of their lives.

From a young age, some children receive pocket money with the freedom to spend it on whatever they please without worrying about what the rest of the month may bring. If a need or want arises during the month, their parents or guardians meet it. This reinforces their reluctance to create and follow a budget.

In most of these cases, the teen is never asked to contribute towards household expenses, even once they get a job. They continue to live with their parents with little to no responsibility and splurge on anything they feel like buying. These money habits were cultivated from a young age and become increasingly difficult to change as the years go by.

Once they move out of the house, these money habits are so deeply ingrained that they struggle to make it work without additional support. The month may start well with them taking care of all their essential expenses, but they tend to run into a bit of trouble by the middle of the month and have to reach out for help.

If your teen has fallen into this trap, don't worry. It's never too late for them to learn the basics. A lot of parents believe that their teens shouldn't need to pay to live with them, and I would agree to some extent. They have every right to live with you, and you shouldn't be making it difficult or impossible. The idea is not for you to rely on their income by taking their entire salary for rent or groceries, but asking them to pay a small portion towards these expenses will teach them responsibility and prepare them for when they move out. Once they start earning a salary, they have the capability to pay rent.

BUDGETING

Whether your teen is at the point where they can start paying rent or not, teaching them about a budget and how to budget is one of the best ways you can sow into their future and set them up for success.

As the opening quote suggests, saving should be a key component of anyone's budget. If you or your teen are not saving something, you need to make a few changes that will enable you to do so. You might be wondering why this is even relevant to your teen at this point in their lives—I'm glad you asked.

By learning how to save from an early age, teens can start building healthy habits that will lead to financial independence as they grow older. Cultivating these habits from a young age is much easier than trying to change their money belief system when they're much older. Not to mention the compound interest they can earn on their savings over the years. We explore this concept in detail in Chapter 2.

It's pivotal for teens to understand the value of money; otherwise, how are they going to spend it responsibly when they're older? To be financially free, independent, and successful, saving money and budgeting should almost be part of their DNA. And when they cultivate a habit of saving, they will be less likely to get into debt later.

Teens should ideally learn how to budget while they are still living at home so that you can help them adjust where necessary. If you're not one for budgeting, now is the time to start.

By creating a budget, you have a clear picture of your income, expected expenses, and where your money actually went.

Looking at your budget at any time during the month should give you a good idea of what you have left after all your expenses are paid. So, if you ever feel like purchasing something on a whim during the month, you can easily refer to your budget to make sure that you have the money to spend without forgetting about that odd bill in the middle of the month or a commitment you forgot you made where you'll be spending money. By tracking expenses, you can also plan better for the next month. If the budget doesn't work the first month, give it time. It takes about three months or so to get the hang of it and account for all expenses, especially the variable ones.

Budgeting mainly consists of four main components: income, expenses, savings and investments, and debt. We'll discuss these elements and some fun activities, budgeting methods, and tips to budget and save. At the end of this chapter, there is a budgeting template that we will work through and that you can use with your teen to help them.

- **Income:** This is quite simple—it's the total amount you receive per month. This could be a salary, allowance or pocket money, any part-time job, birthday money, interest on investments, etc.
- **Expenses:** This is what you spend most of your income on. There are fixed and variable expenses. It's important to keep track of both of these.
    - ▶ Fixed expenses are those that remain constant every month, such as gym membership, rent, car insurance, and car lease payments. They are easy to budget for because you know exactly what you will need to pay monthly.

▶ Variable expenses are monthly expenses that may change from month-to-month, such as groceries, entertainment, and gas. These expenses are harder to budget for because they change, but using a three-month average is a good way to include them in your budget.

- **Savings and investments:** We should always make provisions for savings and investments in our budget. These are as important as your monthly expenses. Without building up savings, how will you take care of emergency costs or go on vacation? We'll explore this concept more in the chapters to come.

- **Debt:** Ideally, your teen shouldn't have any debt at this point, but it's still an important concept to cover because debt is the only way to build up your credit score. A practical way you can help them understand debt is to loan them money to buy something they really want and arrange a payment plan until they have paid it off.

Budgeting Methods

There are various budgeting methods that can be used, and there is no one-size-fits-all. It's best to try them out and see which works best for you (and your teen, as that may be different as well). The three methods we will discuss here are the 50/30/20 rule, the zero-budgeting approach, and paying yourself first. There are a few others, but these are the main ones that most people use.

We will look at these three methods and what they mean. Included under each is also a fun activity you can do with your teen to help them budget.

All of these methods include the four main components of a budget, which we discussed earlier, so they are all valid methods for budgeting. Just like people prefer different forms of exercise, their budgeting preferences also differ.

50/30/20 Rule

This rule is great to use as the initial budgeting method to get your budget started when you don't have a lot of data to go on yet. The rule states that you should allocate 50% of your expenses towards essential ones (i.e., monthly expenses and commitments you have to honor, such as rent and groceries), 30% towards discretionary expenses (like eating at restaurants and buying new clothes), and the remaining 20% should go towards debt repayments if you have any and savings.

Although 50/30/20 is the default way to structure this method, you can use different percentages based on your lifestyle.

A game I love suggesting here is called "Guess the Budget." Give your teen a clean sheet of paper and a pen. Try staying away from the electronics, in case they get smart, and Google the answer. Ask them to write down what they think you as a family spend money on each month. Go through the list and give them a point for every correct entry. Help them to fill in any blanks so that it's comprehensive.

Once you have a list of all the items, ask them to guess how much you spend on each every month. You can decide how to award points here depending on how close they get to the actual number. At the end, you can add up their points and give them a small reward. You can do this every month and challenge them to improve their score.

If you have more than one teen or child, they can all play. Each one should make a list and guess the price. You can reward the one that got the closest on most items.

To relate it to the 50/30/20 rule, you can ask them to allocate each item into a bucket (essential expenses, discretionary expenses, and savings and debt).

Zero-Budgeting Approach

With this method, you start each month on zero, so there are no carryover funds from the previous month. Although you may start at zero with the 50/30/20 budget as well, with this method, there is no prescribed methodology for allocating funds for your budget.

You account for every cent of income, and it is allocated towards something in your budget, balancing to zero at the end. This does not mean that you can't allocate money towards fun things and savings.

An activity you can try here is to give your teen a list of expenses (with figures for the fixed expenses and perhaps ranges for the variable expenses). Give them an income amount and ask them to allocate an appropriate amount to each category until no money is left. They can't go over budget, but they need to use all the money.

You can make it even more fun by having a few jars or containers that represent the various categories and using small items, such as buttons or sweets, to represent the money.

Pay Yourself First

This method follows the quote at the beginning of the chapter. It suggests that you should set money aside to save first and then use whatever is left to cover your monthly expenses. It's important to check how much you need for the essential expenses before making the initial commitment. You need to still be able to make ends meet with the money that is left.

The beauty of this method is that you don't end up saving whatever is left but rather save upfront. A lot of the time, we prefer to spend the money we have left on nice-to-haves instead of saving it. Using this method ensures that you save a portion of your income every month.

A great activity for this one is an online game called *Build Your Stax*. The game takes between 20 and 30 minutes, and what you need to do is invest your initial capital (which is $1,000) in stocks, bonds, and so on to see how much savings you can accumulate in 20 years. Don't worry; the game doesn't last for 20 years. Each minute in the game equals one year.

Here's the catch: in addition to making smart choices with investments, which we will discuss later in the book as well, they will need to use their money every now and then to fix something like the car breaking down. This also teaches them about an emergency fund and why that's important.

All in all, this game is amazing and covers a lot of the basics.

Budgeting Guidelines and Tips

Here are a few guidelines and tips to get your teen into budgeting and managing their money responsibly.

- **Give them an allowance:** This is especially relevant if they don't have a part-time job. By giving them an allowance, you can start teaching them how to manage the little they have and make it a habit before they are exposed to a larger income. You don't have to just give them an allowance; they can earn it through performing chores.

- **Limit spending:** Before they make a purchase, make sure they've thought it through and they're not acting on impulse. It may have been cute when they were smaller, but as they grow older, they need to learn how to limit their spending and be money-savvy.

- **Prevent overspending through peer pressure:** One of the biggest lessons they will need to learn is to not allow peer pressure to push them towards spending more money than they should on something. It's easy to fall into this trap when everyone has the newest iPhone or Converse or when their friends want to go watch a movie, but they've spent their entertainment budget. It's never a good idea to dip into other buckets. We create a budget for a reason.

- **Learn from mistakes:** When they've made a mistake, talk through it with them and ask them what they think they could have done differently to prevent it in the future. You can even share similar mistakes you made in the past to show them that it's okay.

- **Use budgeting templates:** You don't have to create a budget from scratch. You can use an existing budgeting template and adjust it based on your and your teen's needs. There are thousands of options online that you can use. I have also included one in the activity at the end of this chapter.

- **Make adjustments:** Once the budget has been set up, it's important to make room for adjustments when needed. If they suddenly have a new expense or additional income, the budget needs to change. They may also need to make adjustments throughout the month if there are any unexpected expenses and no budget to account for them. Help them with these adjustments and explain why it's necessary.

- **Teach them to save, then spend:** This has been the central theme throughout this chapter. They need to learn to save, but it's important that they also understand how to spend. Saving everything is also not a way to live. We need to make provisions for fun if the budget allows it. If it's a case of either saving money or having money allocated towards entertainment, they can always switch between the two. The first month can be a savings month and the second month an entertainment month, and they can switch between the two.

- **Understand cash flow:** Simply put, cash flow is the money coming in and going out. Money coming in should always exceed the money going out. This will only be an issue if they have credit cards, where they might overspend. It might sound like an obvious thing to understand, but teach them the concept of cash flow now. They should never get into a situation where their expenses are more than their income.

- **Track spending:** Teach them how to record every purchase they make. Tracking spending helps us to create a more accurate budget and shows us where the money went. If there are any issues with the budget or they need to save money somewhere, it will be easier to identify where the unnecessary expenses lie if everything is recorded.

- **Wants versus needs:** They need to understand the difference between wants and needs. Use your own budget for this exercise and ask them to identify what they think are wants and what are needs. Needs should be taken care of first, but wants are still important. We need to make space for that in our budget; however, whenever there is a need for budget cuts, we start with the wants. You can always add them back into the budget once things get better.

- **Pen and paper approach:** Don't be afraid to try the old pen-and-paper approach to budgeting. Every person has their preference, and if your teen prefers a pen and paper (or you, for that matter), don't feel pressured to use technology just because everyone else does.

- **Meet monthly:** Have a recurrent monthly meeting to discuss their budget and talk through any challenges they may have had. Identify any red flags that they might need to pay close attention to the next month. You can even ask them to help with the household budget to give them more exposure.

Using Budgeting Apps

If your teen enjoys being on their phone, like 99% of all teens, you might want to consider introducing them to a budgeting app. There are quite a few of these on the market that you can try out. Have a look around and choose the one your teen will enjoy the most. The app you choose will depend on your and your teen's needs and what you would like to get out of the app.

Some features you may want to look out for in these apps include:

- A spending account linked to the budgeting app
    - Where there is an account linked, check the monthly account fees and transaction fees

    ○   Spending limits on the account

- Savings jar or account where they can store their savings
- Parental monitoring, which will allow you to track the expenses from your phone and access their transaction history
- FDIC insurance
- Automatic categorization of expenses
- Ability to track and categorize all expenses (if not done automatically)
- Data analytics, including graphs or charts that provide financial insights
- Easy access across different devices
- Goal-setting and tracking
- Creating a budget
- Educational content and support

One app may not have all these features, so you should decide which features are most important to you and your teen and look for an app that ticks most of those boxes. Look for something with a user-friendly interface that makes it easy to use the app. The apps that are difficult to use are not more sophisticated—that's a common misconception.

Choose something that is easy to use, meets your needs, is compatible with the devices you have, and offers security measures to protect your money and information.

SAVINGS

Saving is an important part of a budget. Not only physically saving money in an account but also finding ways to save money within your budget, like making smart spending decisions.

Knowing how to save is the difference between financial freedom and feeling like money controls you. There are many other things that play a role and that can help you reach financial freedom, but if you don't know how to save, you might end up spending all of it before you can even enjoy it. Saving helps us to become financially independent and to use money as a tool instead of allowing it to dictate how we live our lives.

Here are some guidelines that can help you and your teen with this concept:

- **Set a savings goal:** Helping your teen to set a savings goal will motivate them to work towards it. Without a savings goal, it may be difficult to consistently save. As humans, we like having something to work towards— something that can propel us forward when our motivation starts to dwindle. That's exactly what a savings goal can do. You can motivate them even more by committing to matching the amount they saved once they reach their goal.

- **Try a "fun money" budget:** This means that you include a category for fun in the budget for them to spend on whatever they feel like. They might be more willing to try it out when they know you're not trying to remove all the fun. We will discuss this further in the activity portion of this chapter.

- **Track spending:** Show them how to record every purchase they make and challenge them to find alternatives that may be cheaper. The next time they need to make the same purchase, they will know where to find it. Tracking their spending may also help to identify places where they could save money, like making coffee at home instead of purchasing coffee every morning. This was already briefly discussed earlier in this chapter.

- **Encourage them to think before they spend:** We've all spent some money impulsively, and every budget should make space to indulge every now and then, but this shouldn't be the norm. Teach your teen to think before they spend money, especially on impulse buys. A great habit to form is not to make any impulse buys but to spend at least 24 hours thinking about it. Ideally, all purchases should be planned and saved for, but we know there are situations where we all like to treat ourselves. Make sure they at least think it over before making the purchase. Having a soundboard, like yourself, to talk through the reasons they think it's a good idea to purchase is an excellent way to curb unnecessary spending.

- **Help with job hunting:** There's nothing better than the feeling of receiving your first paycheck. Depending on your teen's age, they might be able to start working part-time over weekends. Help them to find something they will enjoy, and that can teach them responsibility. We'll discuss this further in Chapter 4.

- **Shop secondhand:** Some of the best purchases I've made have been secondhand. Although it's not always better, you can find amazing deals on furniture, clothes, and even digital devices. Encourage your teen to try out some thrift stores or even online stores like eBay before they buy something new. They might be surprised at what they find.

An activity you can try with your teen to help them think strategically about their spending is to give them a household expense you think you can save money on (like certain food items or gas for the car) and ask them to look around for the best deal. You can reward them by giving them savings for the first month or a commission. This might motivate them to ask for more responsibility next month and help them get into the habit of looking for the best deal.

ACTIVITY

For the first activity, I have included a sample worksheet that you can use with your teen to create a budget. This worksheet is specifically designed for teens with little to no responsibility, so you may need to adapt it when they start paying rent, groceries, etc.

This worksheet also makes provisions to set some financial goals that will help with saving. I have included some examples under each category as well as the goals just to relay the idea of the worksheet, but feel free to change whatever is not relevant.

- The first portion is dedicated to their income. This is self-explanatory. You can add or remove entries here and make sure they cover every source of income. The category "other" could be used for any other income, such as birthday money.
- The next section is dedicated to spending. The following categories have been included, but feel free to add more:
  - Savings
  - Transportation
  - The "fun" budget
  - Personal expenses
  - Giving back

- ○ Other
- The last section is for financial goals: short-term, medium-term, and long-term.
  - ○ Short-term goals are goals you want to reach within the next year.
  - ○ Medium-term goals range from one to five years.
  - ○ Long-term goals are goals you want to achieve after

Budget Worksheet

Month:

Money I receive

Monthly Spending

Financial goals

Short-term goals (One year)
Find a weekend job
Go for music lessons: drums

Medium-term goals (One to five years)
Buy my own drum set.
Buy a car.

Long-term goals (Five years or more)
Finish University and get a good job.
Save money for a down payment on my own house.

SUMMARY

- Following Warren Buffet's advice to save first and then spend money is one of the best pieces of advice you can give to your teen.

- Creating an effective budget is key to managing finances and creating healthy money habits.

- You can promote financial independence in your teen by introducing them to budgeting and saving now.

- A budget consists of income, expenses, savings and investments, and debt repayment.

- Giving your teen an allowance and teaching them how to use it responsibly will help them when they start earning a bigger salary.

Hopefully, the content of this chapter has excited your teen (and you!) to start budgeting and saving. If this chapter didn't convince you to save, I have no doubt the next chapter will. Chapter 2 deals with the effect compound interest has on your savings balance and how you can take advantage of it.

Chapter 2

Discovering the Power of Compound Interest

> *"Compound interest is the snowball effect of money."*
> — **Suze Orman** —

You can earn interest on any positive balance in your bank account, whether it's simple or compound interest. With compound interest, your money grows exponentially because the interest is calculated on the total amount, i.e., initial plus interest. So you can earn interest on interest earned. This means that the longer your money is deposited, the more interest you will earn on your interest, and the more your money will grow.

It may seem like a complex term to understand, but it is quite simple. I have included an example below between simple and compound interest to show the difference. We will use the example of depositing $5,000 over five years, with no additional deposits in between. We will assume an interest rate of 5% for both the simple and compound interest.

With simple interest, you only earn interest on the initial amount that was deposited.

- Year 1: $5,000 + 5% of $5,000 ($250) = $5,250
- Year 2: $5,250 + 5% of $5,000 ($250) = $5,500
- Year 3: $5,500 + 5% of $5,000 ($250) = $5,750
- Year 4: $5,750 + 5% of $5,000 ($250) = $6,000
- Year 5: $6,000 + 5% of $5,000 ($250) = $6,250
- After five years, you've earned $1,250 in interest.

With compound interest, you earn interest on the current amount and not the initial deposit.

- Year 1: $5,000 + 5% of $5,000 ($250) = $5,250
- Year 2: $5,250 + 5% of $5,250 ($262.50) = $5,512.50
- Year 3: $5,512.50 + 5% of $5,512.50 ($275.63) = $5,788.13
- Year 4: $5,788.13 + 5% of $5,788.13 ($289.41) = $6,077.53
- Year 5: $6,077.53 + 5% of $6,077.53 ($303.88) = $6,381.41
- After five years, you've earned $1,381.41 in interest, which is $131.41 more than simple interest.

This might not seem like a big deal after five years; however, if you invested this same amount at the same rate for 30 years, you would have earned $7,500 in simple interest and $16,609.71 in compound interest. That's a difference worth talking about!

Interest can be compounded monthly or annually. In the above examples, the interest is added annually, but interest can be compounded at more frequent intervals. Even if the interest is compounded more frequently, the overall annual interest rate will remain the same.

The longer you invest or save the money, the more interest you will earn. Some people invest for income and withdraw the interest; however, if you want to take advantage of compound interest, no withdrawals should be made. Even investing a small amount early will pay off in years to come. If your teen starts investing now with compound interest and only withdraws upon retirement, imagine the sum they will accumulate by then—especially if they make additional deposits throughout the years.

EXPLAINING COMPOUND INTEREST

Although the above explanation and calculations may seem easy to us, they can be quite complicated for teens. Here are some ways to help you explain compound interest to your teen if the above doesn't quite hit the mark.

It's a Game

Everybody enjoys games! You can play this game over a few months. It involves money, so I'm sure your teen will be interested.

Start by giving them $10 the first month and doubling it every month. However, there are rules to this game.

- They can choose to spend their money at any time; however, even if they spend a portion of it, the compounding effect will stop.
- The first month, they get $10.
- If they manage to save the $10 and not spend it, they get another $10 the second month. Now they have $20.
- If they keep the $20 for another month, you double that. So, after month three, they will have $40.

- I would suggest playing this game for about six months, which will look like this:
  - Month 1: $10
  - Month 2: $20
  - Month 3: $40
  - Month 4: $80
  - Month 5: $160
  - Month 6: $320
- You can adjust the amounts based on what you can afford using the same methodology.

During this period, resist the urge to give your teen any additional money they ask for unless they worked for it. Remind them that they can use the money they have saved; however, it will stop the compounding immediately. This will force them to really consider what they spend their money on and whether it really is a necessity. You can still cover their needs, such as toiletries, but don't give in to any unnecessary spending.

This is an excellent way to teach them healthy saving habits.

Use the Storytelling Method

One of the easiest ways to get some people to understand and remember a concept is to incorporate it into a story. There are a few metaphors you can use here, but the most popular and probably easiest one is a snowball rolling down a hill. Some people even refer to compound interest as the snowball effect.

How does a snowball start? Someone creates a small little ball with snow. The only way to make it grow is to add more snow. If you take your snowball and propel it down a hill, it will gradually get bigger and bigger as more snow is added to the snowball. The longer the snowball is allowed to roll down the hill, the bigger the snowball gets, and the faster more snow is added.

This is exactly what happens with compound interest. The investment might start small, but the longer the money is invested and the more additional payments or interest is accumulated, the faster and bigger it grows.

Make It Practical for Them

While some teens might enjoy the game or understand the story, others need a more practical example to compare it to.

You can use any example that you feel most relates to them, based on what they're interested in. Below are some examples you can use and compare to compound interest.

- If they enjoy working out, ask them how difficult it was in the beginning and how long it took to see results. If they are still new to it, you can explain that it may be difficult in the beginning and results won't show immediately, but the more you keep at it, the more benefits you will reap from it—like feeling more energized, sleeping better, and your clothes fitting better.

- If they enjoy reading, explain to them that when you consistently read for a few pages a day, you make good progress on your book and can finish quite a few books within a year.

- If they like playing video games, you can use this as an example as well, especially for quest or build-type games. The longer you play and the more consistent you are, the more experience you build up to eventually finish the game.

TIPS TO GET THE MOST OUT OF COMPOUND INTEREST

Compound interest is one of the best-kept secrets that everyone is talking about, but no one actually takes advantage of it. It sounds like it's too good to be true, but it exists and is completely legal. Let's look at a few things you can do and discuss with your teen to help them get the most out of compound interest.

Time Is Your Friend

Every example and explanation we have gone through has highlighted the importance of starting as early as possible. If you haven't started saving through compound interest for your teen already, now is a good time to make that deposit.

As we've seen, the longer an amount is invested, the more you benefit from compound interest. Making regular contributions can definitely help, but the biggest factor is the amount of time between investing and withdrawing.

Depending on how long you've been accumulating compound interest, just one year can make a big difference. The first year might seem like a small difference, but by the time you get to year 15 or so, a year's worth of interest may be more than the amount you initially deposited.

Unfortunately, the same is true when borrowing money—which is also an important thing for teens to understand. The longer you take to pay off the debt, the more you end up paying. Once they understand compound interest, the thought that they might be the ones paying it instead of receiving it should be enough to deter them from getting into too much debt. There are good and bad debt, and we'll discuss that in later chapters, but debt is something that should be thoroughly considered and not something done on a whim.

Make Use of High-Yield Savings Accounts

A high-yield savings account has a higher annual percentage yield (APY) when compared with other savings accounts. You will receive more interest and have a bigger balance at the end of the investment period.

These savings accounts tend to be offered by online banks rather than brick-and-mortar banks. Like most other savings and investment accounts, they might have a minimum deposit and balance requirement but offer lower monthly fees and higher APY.

Pay Attention to the Fees

An annual management fee of 2% might not sound like much, but it can have a massive effect on the investment balance. It's important to shop around for the best deals when it comes to investment management fees.

You can't avoid these fees completely, but it's important to get as low a rate as you can. These management fees can end up being more than your returns, which defeats the purpose of investing.

Everything depends on your initial investment and compound interest rate; however, let's look at a simple example of a 2% annual management fee versus a 0.5% annual management fee.

- An initial investment of $10,000.00 at a 5% annual compound interest rate.

- After 30 years, with a 2% annual management fee, the total value would be $43,219.42, with the returns adding up to $24,272.62 while the fees add up to $18,946.80.

- With a 0.5% annual management fee, the total value would still be $43,219.42 after 30 years. However, the returns add up to $37,453.18, and fees up to $5,766.24.

- That's a difference of $13,180.56 in fees!

Contribute Consistently

It's not so much about the amount you contribute. As we've seen, the smallest deposit can lead to some big numbers over the years, and that was with a single contribution. Imagine the difference it would make if you consistently contributed a small additional amount monthly.

If we use the same example, we looked at the beginning of the chapter with an initial deposit of $5,000 with an annual compounding interest rate of 5% and a monthly deposit of $100, the total balance after year 5 would be $13,192, which is already more than what was in the account after year 30 above.

These initial and subsequent deposits are just for illustration purposes. Depending on the investment or savings account you choose, they may have minimum deposit amounts you need to stick to.

Reinvest at Every Opportunity

Most compound savings and investment accounts automatically reinvest the interest earned to increase the balance; however, some accounts might offer a payout at some point or once the investment has reached maturity. The intention should be to reinvest any payouts or dividends back into the investment to earn even more interest.

COMPOUND INTEREST IS NOT ALWAYS GOOD

All of this might sound amazing, and it is. However, as we discussed earlier, compound interest can reveal its dark side when we borrow money.

Most debts use compound interest, which means that the longer there is an outstanding balance, the more interest you end up paying. This effect of compound interest can make it harder to get out of debt.

With most personal loans and credit cards, interest is typically added monthly (compounded daily, in most cases). When we only make the minimum payment, it may not cover all the interest accrued for that month, causing the balance to grow and resulting in more interest charges in subsequent months.

Educate your teen to ensure they make compound interest work for them through investments and not against them through debt. We discuss debt and overcoming or avoiding it in the next chapter.

ACTIVITY

This activity is one of my favorites because, while it perfectly demonstrates how compound interest works, it also showcases the benefits of patience and delayed gratification, and it's fun!

Start by asking your teen whether they would prefer to receive 10 cents now and have the amount double daily for 30 days or receive $1 million once off. If they don't understand compound interest or they easily submit to instant gratification, they will most likely choose the $1 million. You can then either challenge them to go for the other option or show them why the other option is better.

Just like the snowball, it starts slow and takes a while to build momentum, but over time (before the 30 days are up), it will surpass the $1 million. Give them a piece of paper, a pen, and a calculator to do the calculations over 30 days. I have started the calculations below up to day 10 and then skipped to day 30, just to give you a general idea. If you prefer, you can even start with a penny. They will still end up with more than $1 million.

- Day 1: $0.10
- Day 2: $0.20
- Day 3: $0.40
- Day 4: $0.80
- Day 5: $1.60
- Day 6: $3.20
- Day 7: $6.40
- Day 8: $12.80
- Day 9: $25.60
- Day 10: $51.20
- Day 30: $53,687,091.20

In reality, your investment won't double daily (or even monthly), but it's a good way to explain the concept and make sure it sticks. It shows that time and patience can yield better results than giving in to instant gratification.

Summary

- Compound interest is when interest is calculated on the initial deposit as well as the accumulated interest, which leads to exponential growth over time.

- Simple interest is when interest is only calculated on the initial deposit. Any interest earned is not taken into account.

- To help your teen maximize compound interest, encourage them to start early, use high-yield accounts and accounts with minimal fees, and contribute additional amounts when they can. If they receive any interest, they should reinvest it instead of spending the money.

- Compound interest can also be bad. Most debts use compound interest. This is why it takes so long to get out of debt once you've fallen into that trap.

Now that we've discussed compound interest on savings and investments let's move over to debt. We'll discuss good debt and bad debt and how teens can use their credit cards responsibly. We want to help them avoid unnecessary debt that will put them in a financial crisis.

Chapter 3

Overcoming Debt Stress

*"Every time you borrow money,
you're robbing your future self."*
— **Nathan Morris** —

Falling into the debt trap is easy—too easy! This is why it's essential to teach teens about debt, how to manage it, and ways to avoid (or at least limit) bad debt. This quote by Nathan Morris is one of my favorites to use when explaining the consequences of debt to others.

It's easy to worry about and fix the problem now by creating debt; however, we rarely think about the consequences and leave it to our future selves to deal with. The problem is that you have no idea what your future self will be dealing with in a few months or years from now, and trapping yourself with a mountain of debt might be the worst thing you can do.

We all get into a pickle sometimes and need money. But that's why healthy money habits are so important. We need to prepare for these expenses by having insurance, building an emergency fund, and having other savings on standby. We will explore these concepts in later chapters. For now, let's dive a little deeper into debt, what it means, when it can be good, and how to manage it effectively.

GOOD VERSUS BAD DEBT

It sounds strange to refer to debt as good or bad, but there are distinctions. Some debt can help you build your credit record, elevate your credit score, and improve your financial status. However, even good debt can be bad debt if you can't afford it. Just because it's classified as good debt does not mean that it's always a good idea.

Before getting into any debt, it's important to evaluate your financial situation, the need for the debt, and any possible alternatives before committing to it.

With that being said, we have categorized different types of debt into four categories: Good debt, on-the-fence debt, mostly bad debt, and the ultimate bad debt. The reasons for being good or bad have nothing to do with what is acceptable or not, but how it can affect us. For example, credit cards are considered bad debt; however, most people have a credit card. When used wisely, a credit card can be a great tool.

A simple way to remember whether debt is categorized as good or bad is to remember that good debt will help you to make more money in the future, while bad debt only costs you more money.

Good Debt

There are two main types that we will look at here: student loans and business loans.

Student loans can be amazing investments for the future, leading to a higher earning potential and more career choices.

A student loan allows students to further their studies if they don't have the money immediately to do it. However, a student loan should be the last resort. They should first explore grants, scholarships, etc., before resorting to a student loan. The amount required could be reduced significantly with some of the other options.

An additional consideration here is to ensure that they are likely to find a job in that field once they finish studying. Getting a degree for the sake of having one might not be the best way to make debt. In that case, getting a student loan can actually be considered bad debt since the degree will not benefit them in the long run.

A business loan is used to start a new business or expand an existing one. If it's a new business, the business plan needs to be foolproof. Getting into debt and then the business failing is the quickest way to put you in a very difficult financial position. Some risks may be worth taking if you can afford to bear the potential consequences.

Many people also choose to get a home loan as an investment and then rent out the property. This is also considered good debt since the tenants will essentially be paying off your loan, and you can make some extra out of it. There are quite a few things to consider here, though, like the initial down payment, transfer costs, and ongoing maintenance costs.

On-The-Fence Debt

The only on-the-fence debt I want to briefly discuss is a mortgage. Most people would classify it as good debt because you stop paying rent and only pay a mortgage, and at the end of it, the house is yours. So, although you are not making any money (which is the definition we used for good debt), you are investing in it for your future.

While you can most likely save for everything else (like education, buying a car, going on holiday, etc.), it's nearly impossible to save and buy house cash unless you've been saving for years or make a lot of money. This makes it almost essential to get a home loan if you want to own your own house.

A good rule of thumb to use when deciding whether you'll be able to sustain the repayment over time is to ensure that the repayment does not exceed roughly 33% of your income. If it exceeds this, you should either look for a different house to buy or wait until you earn more.

Mostly Bad Debt

This may come as a shock to you because most people have them, but a car loan is considered to be mostly bad debt. Although a good investment in terms of being able to transport yourself, the car's value depreciates from the second you buy it. It's not an asset that adds value to your financial worth.

Whenever someone wants to buy a car, I encourage them to save as much as they can to purchase one cash. If your teen looks at used cars, they won't need to save for too long. It's always nice to get a brand new car; however, car loans have quite a high interest rate, and the fact that they depreciate from the time they leave the dealership makes it a semi-bad investment.

It's not all bad. I have also gotten into debt to buy a car before. Would I do it again? Probably not. I have a car that works just fine, and there is no need to get into debt to buy a new one. If you (or your teen) don't have any transport and public transport is not a viable option, getting a car loan might be good. But make sure to shop around for the best car deal and car loan. And make every effort to pay something upfront to reduce the loan amount.

Bad Debt

You should avoid this at all costs if you can help it, only because they can make you spiral very quickly and put you in a very difficult financial position. In this section, we will discuss personal loans and credit cards.

A personal loan is a loan you can get for any personal reason, such as an upcoming holiday, furnishing your home, home renovations, or even refinancing existing debt. It has quite a high interest rate and, although easy to apply for, can become quite a headache over the years. Because they are so easy to get, people end up spending money they don't have, knowing that they can fix it with a quick personal loan.

There are some "good" reasons to apply for a personal loan, such as unexpected illness or other emergencies when you have no other choice. However, one way to avoid having to apply for a personal loan for emergencies is to start an emergency fund and contribute money to it every month. We will discuss this in later chapters.

By far, the debt with the highest interest rate is credit card debt. This is why some people are so against it. You end up paying a ton of interest on an impulse purchase with a credit card. While many credit cards provide an interest-free period for repayment, it may not always be feasible, depending on your spending amount.

The problem with credit cards is that they give you immediate access to money you don't actually have. Without healthy spending habits, you can easily max out the credit card within the first few days or weeks and deal with the aftermath for years to come.

Credit cards can be a great way to improve the credit score so they can be used for good. We will look at healthy credit card habits later in this chapter.

MAKING WISE DEBT DECISIONS

There are a few important questions or aspects to consider before anyone takes out a loan or gets themselves into debt.

- **Cash flow:** What does your cash flow look like? If you had to spend a large amount of money on this, would it result in falling short in the near future or depleting your entire emergency fund without the ability to replenish it? If so, considering a small loan might be the best way.

- **Cash reserves:** Do you have any reserves you would rather dip into instead of getting into debt? Debt should be your last resort. Don't be so focused on saving money that you are scared to use it when you need it. You saved it for a reason.

- **Credit score:** The better your credit score, the better your interest rate might be. If you have a low or no credit score, you can start building it up by taking small loans and managing it properly, i.e., paying on time, paying more than the minimum installment, and so on. We'll discuss credit score and building credit later.

- **Debt-to-income ratio:** Your DTI is considered when applying for a mortgage, and it's a good measure you can use to determine whether you can afford the repayments. You can calculate it by dividing your total debt commitments by your total income and multiplying it by 100 to get a percentage. Anything below 36% is considered a good DTI, and the maximum should be 45%.

- **Future value:** What would this purchase mean in the future? If it holds no real value for your future, it may not be worth it.

- **Importance:** How essential is it? This question becomes especially relevant when it's a large purchase that will tie you down for a few years. Do you really need it, or is it something you want?

- **Repayment:** How do you plan to repay the debt? Can you afford it? Taking on debt is the easy part. The difficulty is repaying it without putting yourself at a disadvantage with high interest rates.

- **Timing:** Do you need it right now? Perhaps it's something that you can save up for until you have enough money instead of getting into debt.

These aspects should not scare you away from taking on debt, but they help to put things into perspective. You have to take a step back and consider all the pros and cons instead of making an impulsive decision. Sometimes, you will work through these aspects and realize you don't really need to take on the debt, and other times, it will remain a good decision.

CREDIT CARD DEBATE

Some people love it, others hate it, but what is the big deal? Why are some people able to have a credit card and not be over-indebted, while others seem to take on more and more credit just to keep things afloat?

A credit card can be your best friend or your worst enemy. It's all about how you treat it. Let's take a quick look at some of the pros and cons and then dive into how you can teach your teen to use it responsibly.

Pros

- You can still exercise control and help them manage their credit. A quick look at the statements will tell you exactly what they spent the money on and better prepare you for conversations you may need to have. With cash, it's a different story. You have no idea what they spend it on.

- It's very convenient. You don't have to worry whether they have cash on them or money in the bank. The credit card can be used for emergencies and online shopping when needed.

- It helps them build up experience and a credit record. Most teens who are deprived of the opportunity to learn tend to be the ones who splurge when they become adults.

Cons

- There is a possibility that they may misuse the credit card, and you will only find out about it weeks later when looking at the statements. A way to curb this is to have a low limit on the card to ensure they can't go overboard. The more they can show that they are trustworthy, the limit can be adjusted.

- They could also rack up large amounts of debt in their teenage years, which they will need to pay back well into adulthood if they are left to their own devices.

- In some instances, parents take a step back and allow their teens to make mistakes. Although it is important that they learn from mistakes, a bad credit score will affect them when it matters most, like applying for a mortgage.

Using It Responsibly

Although the cons make it clear that there may be lifelong consequences, the best thing you can do for your teens is help them build up their experience now and teach them how to use credit cards responsibly from a young age. Here are some tips to help you.

- **Start with a checking account:** If they don't have a checking account yet, start with that. Help them to manage the money they have before introducing them to credit. This will help to teach them good spending and tracking habits in preparation for using a credit card.

- **Give them access to a linked account:** Before letting them go off on their own, give them a credit card that is linked to yours. This will ensure that you can track and limit their spending and have these important conversations early.

- **Pay it off every time:** A credit card can be used to build good credit, but then you need to pay it off every time to prevent falling into the debt trap. If your teen is unable to pay it off, encourage them not to use it and to save instead until they can afford the item they want to purchase.

- **Explain the details to them:** It's your responsibility to explain the ins and outs to them regarding credit. They should understand how the interest works when they need to pay, how to use the card, and what happens should they miss a payment or pay less than the minimum amount.

- **Set appropriate limits:** Start them with a low limit so that they get the hang of using and paying it back. You can gradually increase the limit as they get more familiar (and responsible).

- **Explain why good credit is important:** This is where you explain to them what bad credit does. Tell them that if they don't manage their money well now, it can have lifelong consequences. It may affect their ability to rent an apartment or buy a car later.

- **Have a discussion about interest accruing:** Most credit cards have an interest-free period, which means they won't charge any interest if the credit is paid off within a certain period. Explain the effect interest has on the balance and how quickly it can escalate if they only make the minimum payment every month.

You can explain credit card debt and interest to them using an example. If they've been asking for something expensive, like a new cellphone, ask them whether they still want it. If they say yes, tell them how much it will cost them. For example, the new iPhone is $799. Their response will likely be that they don't have that kind of money. You then tell them that you're happy to buy it for them, but then they have to pay you $11 every month for the next 10 years. That's roughly a 10.5% interest rate, which is more or less what they would experience with a credit card. Explain to them that due to the interest, not only are they stuck with the debt for 10 years, but by the end of it, they would have paid $1,320 back.

If you're ready to support your teen with their own credit card, shop around for the right one. Consider offers from various companies and choose the best one. Consider factors like the interest rate, grace period for zero interest, late fees, and what the billing cycle is like.

When it's time to make a payment, teach your teen how to do it themselves. You can pay most of them online or through a banking app. Encourage them to pay as much as they can every month and not just the minimum payment. It can be very tempting to only pay the minimum amount so that you have more to spend the rest of the month; however, the interest will devour any money paid over if you only pay the minimum payment every time.

TIPS ON DEBT

We will all get into debt in some form or another during our lifetime. The secret is to get out of it as soon as possible. Some debt is unavoidable, like buying a house or catering for emergencies when you don't have an emergency fund, but you can manage it effectively and get back on track in no time.

Paying off debt is not always fun, and it can be a stressful process. We'll look at a few tips on how to get rid of the debt, but not all teens will be as engaged with this part of financial literacy. It's probably the least fun out of all the concepts, but it's a vital skill they need to learn.

A fun way you can encourage them to pay off their debt as soon as possible is to allow them to splurge on something when they make more than the minimum payment. You can even sponsor them if they use all their money to pay off debt and take care of their responsibilities. As they earn more, they can start taking on the role of financing their wants.

Paying off Your Debt Faster

So, you (or your teen) went and got yourselves into some debt, and you need a little extra help to get out of it. That's okay. Debt is not something you should be ashamed of in the sense that it stops you from doing something about it. It's not great, but we all make mistakes. I've had to go through it myself and know how overwhelming it can be.

Here are some tips to help you and your teen pay off debt so that you can stop paying for yesterday's mistakes with today's money.

- **Be honest about your debt:** When things feel a little too real, many of us like to turn a blind eye and pretend it doesn't exist. Unfortunately, when it comes to debt, it will only make the problem worse. You and your teen need to understand this concept. When trying to get out of debt, you need a full picture of exactly what you owe and what the interest rates are on those debts. This picture might be a little frightening, but knowledge is power. The more you know about your current situation, the better you can deal with it.

- **Make additional payments:** We've mentioned this a few times now, but I thought it would be helpful to also include it under the tips. Avoid only paying the minimum and try to allocate extra money towards debt. If you get additional money from somewhere, like a tax rebate, put it towards repaying your debt instead of spending it on other things. To make it easier, explore some debt repayment strategies to really make a dent in your debt.

- **Decide on a strategy to pay it off:** There are a few foolproof methods to systematically pay off debt.

- ○ **50/30/20 rule**: We briefly discussed this method in Chapter 1. If you have a lot of debt, the aim should be to put most of the 20% towards debt repayment instead of savings.

- ○ **Avalanche method:** This method works on the interest rate, focusing on paying off the debt with the highest interest rate first and then moving to the second highest, and so on. This doesn't mean that you completely ignore your other debt. You pay the minimum amount for all debts and then pay extra on the one with the highest interest rate. Once this is paid off, you can take the amount you were paying towards that debt and pay it over to the debt with the second highest interest rate. Once that is paid off, you move along until all your debt is paid off.

- ○ **Snowball method:** This works similarly to the avalanche method, except instead of focusing on the debt with the highest interest rate, you start with your smallest debt (in amount, not interest rate). Once that is paid off, you put all the money you were paying towards this to pay off the next until all your debt is paid.

- **Bring more money:** By starting a side hustle or picking up a part-time job, they can earn more money that can be put towards paying off debt. We'll discuss helping your teen find a job in Chapter 4.

- **Select Autopay:** This is an excellent strategy for those of us who tend to forget when payments are due. By enrolling in Autopay, you can ensure that you are never late with repayments and avoid any late fees.

- **Reach out for help**: Debt can easily overwhelm anyone, and the sooner you reach out for help, the better. Speak to a professional who can help with enrollment in financial relief programs or financial education and restructuring.

- **Restructure debt:** There are a few options here. You can restructure or refinance debt by converting it to a debt or loan with a lower interest rate. You can also consolidate all your debt into a single loan and pay one amount per month. You have to apply for these, and they are subject to review and approval; however, it might be good to consider if you're struggling to make ends meet.

Debt Tracking

Debt tracking is like setting goals and achieving them. When you can see your progress and get a taste of a debt-free life, you feel more motivated to keep going. Debt tracking is an essential component to keeping the momentum and sticking to the debt repayment strategy of your choice.

A visual representation of progress can provide enough dopamine boost to keep you going. Dopamine is the hormone that makes us feel good, and achieving goals is one of the ways we release it. Let's look at some of the creative ways you can track your own debt or show your teen to track theirs.

- **Let's go with Lego:** Who doesn't enjoy building with Lego blocks every now and then? With this debt tracker, you can use a marker to write on the Lego blocks and build a structure, like a house, for every debt or have a different color for the different debt types. One block can represent a set amount, like $50.

Alternatively, you can also choose to go with a Lego set of your choice with a certain amount of pieces and start building your Lego set as you pay off your debt. You might be motivated to pay off your debt even faster so that you can complete it.

- **For the puzzle lovers:** You'll need to build the puzzle and flip it over before you can start, but that just means you get to build it twice. The idea is to count down your debt as you build the puzzle. Write the amounts at the back of the puzzle pieces (in order), and as you pay off your debt, you add the puzzle piece until you've completed the puzzle. Not only will you be debt-free, but you will have an amazing puzzle to show for it. You can even create a custom puzzle that means something to you.

- **Bullet journal:** A bullet journal is such a fun way to keep track of debt. You can get really creative and stay motivated throughout. Dedicate a page for debt and represent each debt on the page. Decide how much each block will represent and draw the relevant number of blocks for each debt. As you pay it off, you can color the blocks or use stickers.

- **Filling a jar:** You can use anything of your choosing to fill a jar, like sand, M&Ms, colored rice, beads, etc. The sky is the limit! Buy a jar for every debt you have and use a sharpie to write on it, or stick some tape on the jar. Write the debt on the jar (like a credit card or personal loan) and create a thermometer for the debt where you can see how close you are to paying it off. Start at 0% up to 100%. You can even add the amount at every step. As you pay off your debt, you add to the jar.

- **Debt thermometer:** Instead of purchasing jars and spending money on that, you can get creative and make your own thermometer from paper or cardboard that you can stick to a wall or cupboard. You can track the debt the same way with the jars, i.e., include the percentage and amount to be paid off and fill out the thermometer however you choose. You may want to color it as you go or use a piece of ribbon to fill it.

- **Get an app:** There are quite a few debt tracker apps that you or your teen can try if they're not too keen on the creative side of things.

You can get really creative with these debt trackers. Maybe you didn't find one you liked, but it may have sparked some ideas for you to create your own.

BUILDING GOOD CREDIT

If your teen wants to apply for a mortgage one day, they need to have a good credit score. If they never get into debt, they can't build a credit score. I know that sounds a little crazy, but a credit score helps creditors assess how likely someone is to repay their debt. The higher their credit score is, the higher the chances are of being approved for bigger loans (like a mortgage). People with a high credit score also get better interest rates on loans.

Helping your teen to build good credit is pivotal to their future financial success. We have already discussed a few elements that will help them build good credit, such as encouraging them to get a job, adding them to your card as an authorized user, helping them navigate the banking landscape, and cultivating healthy spending and saving habits.

Another thing that you need to discuss with them is their credit score and credit reports. Encourage them to download and check their credit report annually (which is provided free of charge once a year) and ensure that everything is captured accurately. The credit report will detail all current debts, any missed payments, and hard inquiries on your profile. A hard inquiry is when an institution views your credit report to view your credit score and history when you apply for credit.

Any defaults or late payments will affect your credit score. The amount of debt you have also negatively affects your credit score. For example, if you pay the minimum amount on your credit card but use the credit again in that month, it might decrease your credit score because you are continuously making more debt and not getting rid of it.

SUMMARY

- There are different types of debt: good debt, on-the-fence debt, mostly bad debt, and bad debt.

- Debt is categorized as good or bad based on whether it provides any future value and whether the return on investment is worth it.

- Effective debt management techniques include assessing cash flow, using savings to pay for expenses instead of borrowing money, regularly checking your credit score, and ensuring affordability before committing to something.

- Credit cards can be useful in building credit, but they must be used responsibly.

- Debt tracking will help to get rid of debt faster. By having a visual representation of the decrease in debt, your teen will remain motivated to see all of it disappear.

Debt can make us spiral very quickly and siphon all our happiness out of us if we don't manage it effectively. Teaching your teen about debt from an early age may help to prevent them from falling into this trap.

Next, we are going to look at helping your teen secure a job, whether part-time or full-time. This will help them have a source of income and help them understand the value of money.

Chapter 4

Securing a Part-Time Job

*"Don't stay in bed unless you can
make money in bed."*

— **George Burns** —

O nce a teen is old enough to work legally, they should be encouraged to find a part-time job. The sooner they start getting into that and taking on the responsibility that comes with having a job, the better their work ethic will be when they step into the adult world.

Although the quote mentions staying in bed, it refers to stepping back and being lazy instead of putting the work in and generating an income. Another famous quote that comes to mind here is that time is money. Every minute we spend doing nothing, someone else is doing something and earning money. In a world full of people waiting for things to happen to them, be the one that makes things happen.

Encouraging your teens to look for a part-time job while they are still young is vital and has many benefits for them. I still remember my first job as a teen. Although I was quite nervous and unsure what to expect, that first paycheck was worth it. It was a small amount, and I definitely would not have been able to pay rent with it, but it made me feel like I accomplished something and that I could be successful.

WHY IT'S IMPORTANT

If you're not sure whether it's a good idea or not, this section should help you. Some parents may feel that they have the ability and capacity to look after their teen financially, so there is no need for them to get a job. It's not about whether you can take care of them or not, but rather about them gaining experience and building a great work ethic. Here are some reasons why your teen needs to get a job:

- **They earn their own money:** This can alleviate the pressures on parents to fund everything their teen wants to do. When they earn an income, they can finance their own social life and purchase what they desire. They might feel like they have more freedom and work on their independence.

- **They get exposed to different kinds of people:** Learning how to deal with and work alongside different people goes a long way. Having a colleague that you struggle to work with can make your workday a lot more difficult. Learning how to deal with different kinds of people early on will give them a head start on managing relationships.

- **They develop an appreciation for money:** Because they earn their own money, they stop taking it for granted. Once you have to pay to repair your cellphone screen, you start taking better care of it to avoid having to pay for repair.

- **A part-time job can spark their interest in the long run:** Deciding what you want to do for the rest of your life is a big decision. By starting part-time, they can get exposure to various environments and different kinds of jobs that they may be interested in.

- **They learn responsibility for adulthood:** Becoming a young adult is already such a big adjustment that the sooner they can start taking on the responsibilities, the easier the transition will be.

- **They realize why it's important to perform well:** Many young adults leave their jobs because of minor inconveniences like the boss expecting them to work 10 minutes later once a week. Getting used to showing up and performing well is essential to success in the workplace.

- **They can work on their soft skills:** Soft skills are what sets people apart, especially in retail and corporate companies. Soft skills are a set of skills that focus on communication and relationship building. Depending on the part-time job, it may give your teen exposure to the importance of polishing their soft skills.

- **They can contribute to the household:** Any additional income into a household can present much-needed financial relief in one way or another.

- **They get used to delayed gratification:** When earning a salary, you have to wait until payday to get and spend your money. By getting a job and earning money, your teen will learn how to be patient and accept delayed gratification as the norm, which will lead to better spending habits as they grow up.

JOB HUNTING 101

There are a few elements that go into helping your teen find and land their first job. The first thing you need to consider is whether your teen is ready. Some people might argue that a teen is ready by the age of 15, but age shouldn't be the only factor you consider here. You need to make sure that your teen has the time for it, is interested in working, and is mature enough to step into the employment realm.

Some signs that your teen may be ready, other than their age, include:

- They start telling you that their allowance isn't enough to get them through the month and they need more.

- They start talking about having their own business and brainstorming ideas with you.

- They are showing interest in purchasing big items that lean more towards a want than a need.

- They may raise the fact that some of their friends have started working and funding their own social excursions and express a desire to do the same.

- They express their desire to spend their money on things they want and stop asking your opinion.

No Experience? No Problem

It may be difficult to find a job without prior experience, but there are ways to navigate this. There are certain jobs, like being a server at a restaurant, where no experience may be required. Unfortunately, most of these jobs are not very enjoyable, and it's important to prepare your teen for this.

They can also look for online jobs like data capturing, tutoring, or doing something in the community where they live, like pet sitting and dog walking.

Other than that, you can leverage the people you know to help get them a job. Perhaps none of your immediate friends have their own company (although that would be ideal), but they might know someone who knows someone. Leaning on existing relationships can help your teen get their foot in the door. You can also encourage your teen to start networking and build relationships with people in your community. People are more likely to appoint someone they know, especially for entry-level jobs.

Help Them Prepare

Managing expectations when it comes to your teen getting their first job is quite important. Some might be under the impression that they will have a desk and corner office with a view, while others will assume their boss will just love them. While these are possibilities, they need to have a clear picture of what it might be like.

When you think your teen is ready for it, you can start at home. Most kids perform chores at home in exchange for an allowance. This provides a strong starting point for teaching them about the benefits of hard work.

Think back to what your first job was like and tell them about it. Share how you felt on your first day, what your responsibilities were, and examples of when you did your job really well. Tell them how it felt and what the aftermath was like. In addition to this, tell them about a time something went wrong, how you navigated it, and what the result was.

Once the groundwork is there, tell them all about your subsequent jobs. You want to get the message across that it was a great starting point, but it wasn't the only job you had. Tell them about the various areas you tried and highlight the good moments—you don't want them to get bored.

Ask your teen what they are most interested in and whether they know more or less what career they want to pursue. If they have a general idea, encourage them to look for an entry-level job in the same field. For example, if they want to be a veterinarian one day, they can apply to be an assistant at the vet's office. If they don't know yet, let them explore the various fields until they find something they like.

Make sure that you chat with them about paychecks and how much they can expect to make at an entry-level job. Discuss possible deductions and taxes with them. We will briefly discuss a pay stub later in the chapter.

I've included some general tips below to help you encourage your teen to get a job:

- Help them to set a goal. Maybe they've been talking about getting a new phone or buying their own car. Or perhaps they're keen to move into their own place with some friends. Set a goal with them to help kick-start the motivation.

- Make sure that you discuss good workplace etiquette with them. This includes dressing appropriately, always being on time, being courteous, etc.

- Use their skills to paint a picture of who they are. By exploring their identity, they might get a better sense of what they might like to do as a career and what they feel they would be good at. Discussing these may help you create a list of potential jobs for them. Things to consider and highlight include:

○ The activities they enjoy doing include arts and crafts, sports, playing games, listening to music, etc.

○ Is there a particular environment that they thrive in? For example, are they a team player, or do they prefer to work alone? Do they enjoy being the center of attention, or are they more of a collaborator with others?

○ Some skills that they wish they were better at, like playing an instrument, being able to speak in front of people, coding, or anything else that sparks their interest but they haven't had the opportunity to explore.

○ Help them identify their strengths and weaknesses. It's always better to focus on your strengths because these are the things you are naturally good at.

○ What does their free time look like? This plays a major role in the type of part-time job they choose. Some require more time than others. Having a clear idea of when they are available to work may narrow down the search for a job.

● Get them excited by helping them create a resume. We look at this more closely in the activity portion of this chapter.

● Preparing them for their first interview is a fundamental step in the process. They might be asked to interview on the spot when asking for vacancies or handing out their resume. Help them prepare by asking some of the most common interview questions:

○ The most common is "Tell me about yourself." In theory, this shouldn't be a difficult question, but most of us struggle with it. What the potential employer is interested in are things like hobbies, what's important to them, what they hope to pursue further, key personality traits, and experience, if any. They use this question to determine whether the potential employee would be a good fit for the current team.

○ They love asking about strengths and weaknesses, if not already included in the above answer.

○ The availability question might also come up, so it's important to discuss this with your teen. They want to ensure that your teen will be able to show up for work when required.

○ Scenario-based questions are popular during an interview because they show the potential employee's problem-solving skills and critical thinking. They might ask about a recent difficult situation (like dealing with a difficult person or doing something wrong) and what was done to rectify the situation. Having a scenario in their back pocket will help them answer this question without getting overwhelmed.

○ Most people tend to ask whether the interviewee has any questions for them. Although it's okay to say no, what makes people really stand out is this question. Those who take the opportunity to ask something show that they have given it some thought and they are really interested in the job. Prompt them to ask something. It can be something specific to the interview, like what are the next steps or by when they will receive feedback, or the company, or even a personal question, like why they enjoy working at the company so much.

If Your Teen Is Still Resistant

Some teens may need a little more motivation than others to get going. Perhaps your teen is ready, and you've worked through the above pointers, but they're not keen to start looking for a job. Or they said all the right things and listened to whatever you had to say, but there's no action. Here are some steps you can take to help them get going.

1. Find the why behind their actions. Speak to them and really try to understand why they are not keen to start working or why they haven't taken any steps to look for a job. Once you understand the reason, it may be easier to find a solution. Perhaps they feel nervous about working or don't know where to start looking. Speak to them about these and try to find a way around it. Later in this chapter, there is a list of jobs for teens that may help you with this conversation.

2. Once you have addressed the reason why, paint a picture of how great it would be for them to earn their own money; they no longer need to rely on you as their parents to give them money for any social events. Sometimes, a little reminder that they will have their own money to spend as they please is enough motivation to get them going.

3. They might wonder how much money we're talking about. Do some research and give them market-related estimates for part-time jobs (ones that you know they might be interested in). Using fast-food restaurants as an example, they pay per hour. If they get $17 an hour and work just 10 hours a week, that's $170 per week, which calculates to $680 per month.

4. Sometimes, we have to make difficult decisions as parents. For this step, I want you to make a list of some of the

optional luxuries your teen currently has (like subscriptions and makeup) and start putting in some family boundaries when it comes to these luxuries. Tell them that they will need to start paying for these if they still want it. It might seem harsh at first, but it may be the only way you can get your teen out there.

Jobs for Teens

There are quite a few jobs that teens can consider. Here are a few ideas for online jobs, general jobs, and jobs for teens who might have social anxiety. Choose the category that would suit your teen best and chat with them about the possibilities.

Best online jobs for teens:

- Data capturing
- Online tutor
- Starting a blog
- Telemarketing

Best general jobs for teens:

- A job in retail
- Babysitting, pet sitting, or house sitting
- Camp counselor
- Golf course caddy
- In the restaurant or food business, such as a server, dishwasher, or cashier
- Library assistant
- Taking care of people's lawns, cutting the grass, basic landscaping, etc.

- Tutor

Jobs for teens with social anxiety:

- Assistant at an animal shelter
- Assistant for a pet groomer
- Cleaner or helping to declutter
- Restaurant staff at the back, i.e., where they don't need to deal with people
- Stocktaking (most retail businesses need a stocker at the back)
- Warehouse packer or stocker

It's a Balancing Act

Balancing school and a part-time job may be challenging for some, but there are ways to make it work. Make sure that they have a clear idea of their schedule and when they are available to work and find a job that will fit into their schedule.

When it's exam time or they have a project, they can always ask their employer whether there is a possibility to adapt their hours. Most employers understand that teens have responsibilities at school and will help to make it work.

With a busy schedule, it's important to remain healthy and stay hydrated. Provide wholesome meals, pack lunch, and make sure they drink enough water during the day.

Above all else, make sure that they still make time for fun. Keep a close eye on them and look for signs of burnout or excessive stress. You want them to take on additional responsibilities, but you also want them to see their friends and have fun now and then.

When It Doesn't Work Out

We've all been rejected for a job. It doesn't always go your way. Getting turned down for a job is part of the process, and your teen might have to go through it. When this happens, acknowledge the pain that they are feeling. Don't try to make them feel like they're being silly for feeling hurt or pretend like it isn't a big deal. To them, it is. Listen to how they're feeling and reassure them that it doesn't define who they are.

Some teens may need some time to work through it, while others bounce back quickly. Wherever your teen is on the spectrum, give them the time and space to grieve. When they're ready, encourage them to try again.

Take time with them to reflect and see whether there is anything they could do differently the next time. Sometimes, there isn't anything, so don't be too focused on finding something. Instead, it might motivate them if they know there is something they can improve on. Maybe it's their interview skills or the way they present themselves. Or maybe they were just not suited for the job they applied for. An extreme introvert with social anxiety will struggle to thrive in a retail job.

Whatever the reasons, help them to bounce back quickly. Resilience is built over the years based on a few aspects, including experiences and a support system. Always be your teen's support system, and let them know that you're their number one fan.

PAY STUBS AND TAXES

Understanding how a pay stub works and how to file taxes are the basics when it comes to employment. Although your teen doesn't need to know any of it, it will make them feel like they are better prepared and informed about their finances. As they get older, these are essential to financial literacy. It's like the concept of compound interest: You don't have to know the details, but you have an immense advantage if you do.

Understanding a Pay Stub

A pay stub contains all the important information about earnings and deductions. It's very similar to a paycheck; however, a pay stub contains more detailed information than a paycheck. Teens need to understand the elements of a pay stub and what to look out for, to ensure that they are compensated correctly.

For most teens, the elements on a pay stub may be foreign. It's one thing to tell them all about it, but it's easiest to understand when they can see how it plays out. If they haven't received a pay stub yet, use one of your old pay stubs to show them the elements and explain each one if you're comfortable doing so. Or find an example online.

In most cases, companies will supply a paycheck or a pay stub. If they only provide a physical paycheck, the pay stub can generally be accessed through the company's online portal, or you (or your teen, if they are the employee) can contact human resources for a copy.

On the pay stub, show and explain the following elements:

- **Pay period:** This could be weekly, biweekly, or monthly. If monthly, it won't necessarily run from the first to the last day of the month; some pay periods start on the 15th, 20th, or 25th. This should be clearly indicated on the pay stub.

- **Hours worked:** This is generally also shown, especially if there is an hourly rate.

- **Gross income:** This is the total income before deductions. It's normally the amount confirmed in the appointment letter (if applicable) or what is discussed during the interview or successful appointment.

- **Year-to-date pay:** Shows the total gross pay to date for the financial year. This is important for tax returns.

- **Net income:** This is the total income after all deductions have been made, i.e., the amount that is paid into your bank account.

- **Federal income taxes:** This is deducted every month or during the pay period to avoid having to pay a large federal tax amount during tax season.

- **FICA tax:** Your employer deducts a portion of your paycheck for Social Security and Medicare taxes, which help fund benefits for retired and disabled individuals. Your employer also contributes an equal amount towards these taxes. While you may not see an immediate benefit, these contributions ensure that when you retire or if you ever become disabled, you will be eligible for Social Security benefits.

- **State tax:** Not applicable to all states; however, where state tax is mandatory, your employer will withhold an amount for state tax.

- **Additional deductions:** These are any additional deductions that the employer will highlight to you, such as insurance, an employee program, a health savings plan, or 401(k) retirement plans.

Every aspect of a pay stub is important, including the employee's personal details, and should be reviewed with each pay period to ensure accuracy. It's especially crucial to verify the hours worked and the deductions taken from the gross pay.

Taxes

Regardless of age, if you earn a certain amount per month, taxes are deducted from your paycheck. Your tax liability depends on the amount you made during the tax year and how it was made. You can only be exempt from tax deductions if you earn below a certain amount or the income received falls within the list of income that is free from tax. This includes gifts, child support, welfare payments, and dividends on life insurance. Most of these won't apply to teens except for gifts.

Taxable income is calculated using the total income for the tax year minus any deductions—including the standard deduction. You can find the standard deduction as well as the tax brackets for the relevant year on the Internal Revenue Service (IRS) website.

The total tax that needs to be paid depends on the tax bracket for taxable income once all deductions have been excluded. The tax brackets are different depending on whether you are filing as a single filer or married.

Tax is calculated on a sliding scale. Let's look at an example of the 2024 tax year. Below is a summarized table of the lower tax brackets for a single filer in 2024 (Allec, 2024):

Taxable Income (single filer)	TaxRate
$0–$11,600	10%
$11,601–$47,150	12%
$47,151–$100,525	22%

If the taxable income is $30,000 (after the standard deduction), the person will fall into the $11,601–$47,150 tax bracket; however, they won't pay 12% on the entire $30,000.

The first $11,600 will be taxed at 10% and then 12% on the remaining $18,400. Their total tax will be $1,160 + $2,208 = $3,368. Remember that these are the annual values. The annual tax liability must be equal to the sum of taxes paid throughout the year. If there is a difference, this is either due by the individual where the amount paid is less or will be refunded if they have paid more than what is required. This will be handled by the IRS.

It is important to take note that each state may have its own taxes, depending on where you live. Ensure that you check the tax requirements for your state before you (or your teen) file taxes. If you're not sure whether your teen needs to file a return, you can use the IRS's interactive online tool (Do I Need to File a Tax Return?, 2024) to find out or check the IRS Publication 501 for the relevant filing year.

ACTIVITY

Creating a resume can be both a daunting and exciting venture for teens. Writing an excellent resume is key to securing a job. Some employers won't even consider someone for an interview if their resume is not up to scratch, regardless of how great they are in person.

A resume should include all the important information that employers may need, such as personal information, experience (if any), and relevant skills. Anything that is not relevant to the job should ideally be excluded. For example, babysitting nieces and nephews may show that they are trustworthy, regardless of whether the job being applied for is babysitting.

Help your teen create a resume by using the below template and talking through the sections. You can even give them the template and ask them to complete it themselves and do a final review before it's printed or sent out. Check for any spelling or grammar mistakes. It's okay to explore with font sizes, but the font used should be professional. No curly or fun font. Times New Roman or Arial works best for a resume.

Resume Template

Name Surname

[Address] [Phone number] [Email]

Professional Summary

Include a few sentences highlighting any relevant skills, education, awards or certificates of achievement, and interests.

Education

If your teen has already graduated, the year of graduation and the name of the school can be included. Alternatively, they can list the school, their current grade, and subjects.

Experience

If this is their first job, you can remove this portion. If they have any previous work experience, they can include it here.

[Date from] - [to]

[Company name], [Job title], [Job position]

[Key responsibilities]

Volunteer experience

If they don't have professional work experience but have some volunteer experience, they can add the details here. They can include the organization's name, the role they fulfilled, dates, and a summary of what they helped with.

Key Skills

A list of their strengths, focusing on skills that may be relevant to the position they are applying for.

Keeping the resume clean and neat will make it stand out.

SUMMARY

- By encouraging your teen to get a job, they will build a strong work ethic, independence, and an appreciation for the money they earn.

- Having a job comes with several advantages, such as earning one's own income, gaining experience in working with a diverse group of individuals, and developing a sense of responsibility.

- Look for signs that your teen is ready to work part-time.

- If they don't have any experience, use networking to get their foot in the door or look for jobs where no experience is required.

- Help them build resilience by supporting them through job rejections and helping them get back out there.

- Go through the elements of a pay stub with them and answer any questions they may have.

Getting them on board may be a challenge at first, but once they get into it, they will quickly learn how to navigate this new world. We all had to start somewhere.

Now that your teen is well on their way to finding their first job let's discuss the importance of insurance and how to help them protect their money from unexpected events.

Chapter 5

Safeguarding Your Money From Emergency Situations

"When you're young, fit, and full of drive, it's easy to think that 'it will never happen to me.' But this is the myth of invincibility."

— **DBS Singapore**

Teens don't get much exposure to insurance when they're young. They are left to figure it out for themselves as adults, sometimes when it's too late. Insurance and its importance should be part of their toolkit for becoming financially literate teens. Having insurance for various possibilities helps protect any accumulated savings and investments when something happens.

It's best to prepare them early so that they know the types of insurance they will need to build into their budget as they become older and move out. Some people may feel like insurance is unnecessary, like it's a waste of money because you get nothing in return. The thing is, you should be happy when you get nothing in return. Insurance is there for those in-case moments. When something goes wrong and you need help, your insurance will come to your rescue.

You don't have to make it too complicated for them because they don't need it immediately, but you want them to listen still and understand. Keep it simple. Explain the insurance you have and why, as well as what it covers. If you ever needed to claim for insurance, tell them about the experience and how much different it would have been if you didn't have insurance.

Use real-life examples to explain why insurance is essential. If they buy a car one day, insurance will cover the expenses if they get into an accident or if their car is stolen. If they start a business or buy a house, insurance will cover electrical faults, flooding, and so on. Having insurance on your phone means they will give you the means to buy a new one should anything happen to it. Insurance is a way to keep our belongings safe and safeguard us from accidents.

There are a few essential points that you need to make clear to them regarding insurance before you get into the details.

- Although house and car insurance may be the obvious ones, other types of insurance may be important. When you're traveling abroad, having travel insurance is vital. Your teen should consider taking out insurance for their furry friend as well to save them some costs if their pet needs to be admitted or receive expensive treatment.

- There are various companies that offer different types of insurance, and the key is to shop around for the best deal. Just like anything else, you shouldn't settle for the first offer. At the same time, the cheapest is also not always the best option. Some companies can make their insurance rates cheaper by excluding certain things. Make sure that you read and understand the terms and conditions before signing up for any type of insurance.

- Don't fall into the insurance fraud trap. Tell them about insurance fraud, and although it may seem harmless, it does a lot more damage than they think. Insurance fraud has a ripple effect on premiums for all insurance holders and can lead to becoming unaffordable. Claiming that more damage was done than the reality just to receive a bigger payout, staged collisions, planned accidental damage to appliances, or allowing healthcare professionals to charge for a service that wasn't provided are all examples of insurance fraud.

TYPES OF INSURANCE

As mentioned, there are quite a few types of insurance out there. It's not necessary to have every type of insurance unless you feel like you need it. Here are the most common insurances that may apply to some teens. Perhaps not right now, but somewhere in the near future.

Renters Insurance

There is a difference between renters insurance and home insurance. As the tenant, it's important that you get renters insurance. Home insurance is for the person who owns the property, while renters insurance is for the tenant. The home insurance won't cover the tenant's belongings inside the house or any expenses where the tenant was responsible for the damage.

Some people don't see this as a necessity, but it can save you in a pickle! Accidents and burglaries happen, whether you're prepared for them or not. By having renters insurance, these expenses will be taken care of.

They should get renters insurance as soon as they move out, whether it's into their own apartment or dorm. The insurance may be required by the landlord or residence, but even if it isn't, they should still get it. It protects their possessions in case something happens and covers them if accidents occur, like a running tap causing water damage or their friends accidentally damaging the door.

Renters insurance typically covers the following:

- Liability: This part covers any damage to the property that was the renter's or one of their visitors' fault. It will also cover any costs related to injuries obtained on the property for whatever reason to both the tenant and visitors.

- Home contents: This includes tenant personal items, such as electronic devices, clothes, shoes, furniture, houseware, textbooks, etc. Confirm with the insurance what is covered, especially if your teen has some high-value items or collections. This may require an additional add-on to the insurance.

- Additional expenses: Some renters insurance may even cover hotel stays if the tenant is unable to live in the apartment for a while due to renovations or maintenance. This is not always included and should be carefully considered.

Before shopping around for insurance, help your teen make a list of their personal belongings that they need insured and take a few notes on the apartment or dorm they plan to move into, such as the size of the apartment and any security measures in place, such as an alarm system.

The cost depends on several factors, including the location and any add-ons to the normal insurance policy. It will also differ from company to company, so shop around for the best deal. Most renters insurance comes with a standard deductible payable when a claim is submitted. This should be taken into account when considering the insurance.

If your teen has roommates, they may be able to share the cost of the renter's insurance with them. Inquire about this with the insurer and discuss it with the parents of the other teens. It could save everyone money instead of all of them paying separately.

Car Insurance

There are a few different kinds of car insurance. If the car is financed through a financial institution, there are specific requirements that have to be included in the car insurance.

Only once they have a full driver's permit can they start thinking about getting a car. If they're not quite ready to buy a car but you still want them to experience driving, you may need to add them to your existing car insurance as an additional driver. Give them the responsibility of paying the additional fee applicable so they get used to paying for car insurance.

Car insurance rates are based on several factors, including age, how long you've had your license, any previous car accidents, the type of car, where you live, and how much you drive during the month.

This insurance is non-negotiable if you drive because anything can happen. You can be the best driver in the world and still be involved in a collision because you are not the only driver on the road. Your safety also depends on those around you.

While you can encourage them to be a safe driver and give them tips, you should still discuss what they need to do if they get into an accident. Make sure they are equipped to deal with the situation. It's important they follow these steps:

- If they were lucky and the car didn't stop during the accident, they should stop immediately.

- If they have any serious injuries, they should avoid moving at all and wait until emergency personnel arrive to assist.

- If they are okay and have other people in the car, they should check them for injuries.

- If everyone seems okay and it's safe, they should try to move to the side of the road. Where the car is still running and able to, they should get the car out of the road as well.

- If someone hasn't already done so, it's in their best interest to call the police and emergency services, regardless of how serious the accident was. In some states, it's a legal requirement to involve the police and submit a report where some threshold in terms of damage has been met. This will be required by the insurer when claiming. If they are not sure whether it is required or not, they can ask their insurance company.

- Before they leave the scene, they should exchange personal information with the other driver who was involved in the accident. Details such as their full name, contact number, insurance company, insurance policy number, details of their vehicle (type, model, and color), license plate number, and take a photo of their driver's license. They should also make a note of exactly where the accident happened. Tell them to film the scene or take as many pictures as they can involving the accident and surrounding areas.

  o Pro tip: Add a dash camera to their cars that will capture accidents as and when they occur. This can be very beneficial for insurer claims.

- Once all of this is done, they can call their insurer and start the process of submitting a claim. It doesn't matter whose fault the accident was; the insurers will sort this out and decide who will be liable for the costs.

Health Insurance

Discussing the need for additional health insurance should start at an early age and not just before your teen moves out. Having a health insurance plan can help reduce anxiety if they were to fall ill.

Without healthcare insurance, we tend to delay important check-ups and consultations because we have to pay for them ourselves. This means that any possible issues are only detected much later, which could lead to bigger health issues.

Having additional health insurance and dental coverage will ensure that your teen goes for these non-essential but important check-ups. Perhaps they're still under your insurance at the moment, but you should still discuss this with them and ensure they make provisions for it within their budget. Emphasize the importance of preventative screening and the link to early detection.

There are different types of health insurance plans, each with its own set of benefits and coverage they provide. Help your teen work through the various options and choose the one most suited to them.

- Catastrophic Health Insurance: This insurance offers low coverage and a high deductible. It's designed for the young and healthy who won't mind paying a high deductible when they need coverage.

- Health Maintenance Organization (HMO): With these plans, you have to choose a primary care provider (PCP) within a specific local network and need a referral from the PCP to see a specialist. The premiums tend to be low. You are also restricted to local network hospitals.

- Preferred Provider Organization (PPO): These plans also require you to choose a PCP, but the network is much larger than that of an HMO. The premiums and out-of-pocket expenses are higher than HMOs.

- Point of Service (POS): This is a combination of HMOs and PPOs, requiring a nomination of a PCP and the need for a referral to see a specialist; however, some out-of-network cover may be included.

- Exclusive Provider Organization (EPO): These are similar to HMOs; however, it has a larger local network, and you have to obtain all services required within the network. Any non-emergency services obtained outside of the network may not be covered.

Your teen needs to understand the benefits and any network restrictions on their plan to utilize the health insurance effectively. When it comes to seeking services, they should look for providers within the applicable networks (if needed) and keep any records of the services provided. They should receive a bill, statement, and/or receipt. If there are any issues with the claim, contacting the insurer can help resolve the problem, and they'll need the documentation to query the claim.

ROLE OF INSURANCE IN A RETIREMENT PLAN

It might not be obvious right away, but investing in insurance now can help to build a robust retirement plan for the future. By having insurance, you have the peace of mind that important matters will be taken care of when the unthinkable happens. That means that you don't need to get into debt or use your savings to cover these unexpected expenses.

We will discuss retirement and planning for retirement in the last chapter.

SUMMARY

- Teens often feel like they are invincible and don't need to worry about any type of insurance. This is a myth that you should discuss with your teen.

- Insurance is there for the "what if" moments in life. Explaining what insurance is and why it's important early on will help your teen understand its importance.

- When explaining insurance, keep it simple and use real-life examples that they can relate to.

- Help your teen shop around for the best deals that meet their needs.

Although we have only touched on three major insurances, there are many more that you can discuss with your teen. Once they understand the basics, it will be easier to explain the more complex insurances. In the next chapter, we will look at the basics of investing.

Chapter 6

Planting Seeds of Financial Success Through Investing

> *"Investing should be more like watching paint dry or watching grass grow. If you want excitement, take $800 and go to Las Vegas."*
> — **Paul Samuelson** —

Wealth takes time to build, and there is no shortcut; safe and well-thought-out investments with a clear plan are key to financial success, as are budgeting and saving with the best strategies. Investing is not an extreme sport and may not be exciting in the beginning, but as money begins to grow and you see the fruit of patience, it all becomes worth it.

BASICS OF INVESTING

Investing can be quite complex, and it's easy to lose money or feel like you're wasting your time if you're not sure what you're doing. The growth is supposed to be slow and steady. Any investment that grows quickly comes at a higher risk of losing. High-risk investments should only be considered when necessary and in consultation with a professional who understands the investment market. Even then, there is a huge risk that you can lose everything.

Slow and steady is best, which is why investing as soon as possible yields the best results. For investing, we'll look at the benefits of encouraging your teens to start early, the challenges they may face, and tips for you to help them invest. I've also included a step-by-step guide to get them started.

Why Start Early

It could be difficult to motivate a teen to start investing now if they're not going to pick the fruits of their efforts anytime soon, but there are a few reasons why they should start early. Highlight these to them. If you started investing early, tell them your story and how your investment has grown. If you didn't start early, explain what effect it has had on your investments and how different the picture could have been now. Something is sure to stick.

- **Compound interest:** We discussed this topic in detail in Chapter 2. It is very evident when it comes to investments.

- **It cultivates healthy financial habits:** As soon as a child starts making or receiving money, they start cultivating money habits—whether good or bad. By teaching them to invest some of their money instead of spending it on wants, you are cultivating habits that money can't buy. They will learn early to set money aside for investments and build it into their budget from a young age.

- **Reaching financial freedom:** Most people who didn't start investing early are reliant on their jobs to make any decisions. It might not be a job they want to do for the rest of their life, but they are so financially dependent on their job that they don't have the opportunity to explore other options or pursue their dreams. By having solid investments from a young age, they will be able to base their decisions on creating a better life for themselves.

- **Pique their interest:** Once they really get into investments and understand the hype, they'll be so thankful that you encouraged them to invest early. As soon as they start seeing the effect of consistently investing in all the right places, they will start looking for more ways to invest and grow their portfolio.

- **The possibility of early retirement:** If their investments are doing really well, they may be able to retire early. The sooner they start investing and growing their financial future, the closer they will be to early retirement.

- **They don't have a lot of expenses:** Teens don't have a lot of expenses. There are very few things they need to pay, especially if they're still living with you. This means that they have quite a bit of disposable income that they can allocate towards investments to get a good head start. As they get older, their expenses will increase, and they may not have as much to invest. The earlier they start, the more compound interest will work for them.

- **They have a higher risk tolerance:** Because they are so young, they can take on more risk than someone who is a little older. That's because they have time to recover if they experience any losses, whereas someone who is a little older can't afford to start over.

- **They gain experience:** The sooner they start investing, the more experience they can build up and become one of the best. It's just like any other skill—the more you do it, the more you will learn and the better you will become. They might feel like they're out of their depth for a while, but they will become seasoned investors in no time. They may even have an advantage over their friends who didn't have the opportunity or the means to start investing early.

- **Regret comes too late:** If they don't start now, they may regret it 10 or 15 years from now if they see what their friends have been able to accumulate or they start looking into what they could have had. That regret will be too late. Help them set themselves up now.

Challenges for Teens

Teens may face additional challenges when investing that adults won't necessarily need to overcome. You will need to support your teen through this process to ensure they make a success out of it. It will take a little more handholding than some of the other journeys they embark on. Growing their nest egg from a young age will make such a big difference as they grow older, and they will never be able to thank you enough for the nudge and assistance.

The first challenge is related to opening a brokerage account, which is something they will need if they want to invest. Most brokerage firms require the person opening the account to be at least 18 years of age. If your teen is not 18 yet, you may need to do this for them, but educate them on the process and everything you need to do to open the account.

Probably the biggest challenge they face is the lack of knowledge and experience in the field. They need someone to help them and guide them into making informed decisions. If you don't know much yourself, do some research or try to find an expert that can guide you and your teen. Investing is not something that you can just figure out as you go. It's real money on the line, and it's important to at least understand the basics.

We'll cover some in the remainder of the chapter, but the more you know, the better.

Tips to Help Them Invest

While there is always a risk, sometimes it's worth it. Instead of making them stress out about it, try these tips to get them into investing.

Help Them Understand Investments

Start with the basics of investing. There are certain terms they need to understand before they step into the investing world. This is not an exhaustive list of terms, but it is a good starting point.

- **Bull and bear:** If a market is referred to as a bull market, this means that the prices are rising, whereas a bear market means they are falling. Some people buy and sell stocks based on whether it's a bear or bull market.

- **Buy and hold strategy:** This is a different strategy from the above, where you buy stocks and keep them, regardless of whether the price rises or falls. The aim is to invest and 'forget' about the investment, i.e., you don't check on it often in the hopes that it builds over time. Most of the time, it does.

- **Compound interest:** If you need a quick refresher on this, refer back to Chapter 2.

- **Investment types:** There are different assets you can invest in, such as exchange-traded funds (ETFs), stocks, bonds, real estate, etc.

- **Diversification:** A diverse portfolio is one where your portfolio consists of a collection of various types of investments. This helps to safeguard your money because if one of the assets becomes loss-making, the others can make up for it, and you don't lose all your money. We'll take a deeper dive into diversification later in the chapter.

- **Dollar-cost averaging:** With this strategy, you commit to investing a specific amount into the same asset at regular intervals, regardless of whether the asset improved or declined in value.

- **Risk and return:** Any investment comes with risk. As a general rule of thumb, the higher the risk, the higher the return. However, with higher risk comes a bigger chance of losing everything in a heartbeat. It's important to decide what risk appetite you have before investing in high-risk investments.

Make It Fun

There are a few ways you can make investing fun for your teen. Here are some ideas.

- **Play a game:** This works really well with younger teens and those who seem less interested in investing at the moment. Sometimes, all it takes is to see the potential of investing. Playing a game where no real money is involved can be the little push they need to understand and change their mind about committing. A great game to try is "Monopoly," which can teach the basics of investing and dealing with money. When playing, put an emphasis on these concepts and challenge them to think differently than what they normally do when playing the game. There are a few online simulation games that you can try as well, like Wall Street Survivor or Stock Market Game, where they can pretend to invest in certain stocks and see how they do.

- **Fire up their competitive side:** You can always make a competition out of it. If you have more than one teen, they can compete against each other, or you can compete against your teen. No one needs to invest any actual money, but they should be challenged to choose a stock and see whose stock performs the best over a set period. Track the stocks together and discuss any changes. This will teach them what to look out for. Maybe you can encourage them to check out some of their favorite brands on the stock market, like a fast-food chain or a brand they love.

- **Get them involved:** If you have active investments and you feel comfortable sharing the details with them, show them how the investment is doing. Share details such as when you started, how it has been performing, and any changes you've made. When they have a bit of understanding of how it works, you can always let them choose a stock, buy a small amount, and track it together.

- **Praise and reward:** If they learn something new or are able to explain changes in stocks without your help, praise and reward them for getting it right (or trying, at least). If there are any gaps, help to fill them and encourage your teen to learn more.

Where to Invest

This might be one of the hardest parts of investing—knowing where to invest. There are quite a few options available to them, and we will discuss this in detail later in this chapter.

Fees Associated With Investing

Some types of investment have their own investment fee, which will affect returns. Your teen should do adequate research and understand all fees related to the investment and how it will affect their investment. If they choose to use a professional to help them, this is an additional fee that should be taken into account.

Make sure they compare fees for the various investment types and choose the best option for them. Those investments that are managed by a fund manager tend to have higher fees than ETFs that track an index like the S&P 500.

Understanding the Risks

We briefly discussed risk and reward earlier, but it's important to go into a bit of detail on the possible risks that one takes when investing. Although you want to encourage your teen to invest so they can reap the rewards, highlighting the potential risks is just as important.

- **Risk of losing:** This risk will always exist, regardless of how stable the investment is. Doing proper research on the stock and understanding historical trends is important, especially if the idea is to invest and forget. To mitigate the risk of losing everything, encourage them to diversify their portfolio while still having notable investments. Another great rule of thumb here is to only invest the money you know you'll be okay to lose.

- **Too good to be true:** There are investments that seem too good to be true, and they are. Explain the dangers of investing with unauthorized providers and nudge them to ask for a second opinion if they're not sure. If they are ever pushed by someone to make an investment immediately before they can even review the details, this should be a major red flag.

- **"Shiny objects:"** Warn your teen against the "shiny objects" risk that most new investors fall victim to. This is when investors choose to invest in the newest fad or hyped investments without understanding the risk or potential value of the investment. The investment might not be as great as everyone is making it out to be or may not fit into your teen's risk profile. In both cases, this would be a bad investment decision. Encourage them to research potential investments properly before making a decision, regardless of who endorses the investment.

STEPS TO START

Once they have the basics down, you can look at getting them started. If they're not ready yet, take them through the steps anyway to ensure they are prepared when the day comes. There are several factors they need to take into account when getting started.

Step 1: They should start by gaining some basic knowledge of stocks and other investments. This knowledge will help ensure that they don't lose their money in the first week. Understanding the fundamentals and staying up-to-date is crucial; however, they should also be careful which sources they reference.

Sources like TeenVestor.com and Investor.gov are great sites with free educational content for teens and beginner investors. There are also some great online courses for all ages.

Step 2: Setting financial or investment goals will help to have something to work towards. Perhaps they want to start saving for a down payment on a house, buy their own car, or go on holiday with friends. Help them set realistic and relevant goals they want to chase with the growth of their investments.

Step 3: Not all investment types may be appropriate for teens, so the next step is to find the right types of investments. Regardless of the type of investment, if they are younger than 18, they still need the help of a parent to open their brokerage account and/or manage their investments.

Some of the best investments for teens are exchange-traded funds (ETF), certain stocks, and US saving bonds.

- ETFs are on a lower scale when it comes to risk, but that also means that the reward is lower. It is a great starting point, though, and it is smart to include some ETFs in their portfolio. ETFs can be traded like stocks through an online broker but operate more like mutual funds, which makes them more stable and less risky. It's like investing in a collection of stocks. Investing in ETFs means that you already have quite a diverse portfolio. The most well-known ETFs include NASDAQ (stock symbol: QQQ), Dow Jones Industrial Average (stock symbol: DIA), and The S&P 500 (stock symbols: SPY, VOO, and IVV).

- When it comes to stocks, choosing something they are interested in could help kick-start the process. Help them find stocks that they can relate to, such as brands they know and love, companies that tie in with their hobbies, or even companies that some of their relatives (or even you) work for. Although they may not all be the best companies to invest in, your teen may find it interesting to track their performance and be able to make better-informed decisions about investments.

- A safe way for a teen to invest is through US saving bonds; however, these are more for saving purposes than trying to grow your money. These are essentially loans you make to the government, and they reward you by paying back the amount with some interest. These bonds can extend up to 30 years.

Step 4: Once they know more or less where they want to invest, they should do additional research into the company they wish to invest in. The first thing they should look at is the company's annual report. This report includes crucial information about the company's performance and other corporate information that may be of relevance to investors. Some companies may release a 10-K report instead of an annual report; however, they serve the same purpose and have much of the same information in it.

Step 5: This is where it gets very interesting. Now, it's time to look at the company's financial data relative to its competitors. There is no need for your teen to use the annual report and determine it themselves; they can utilize one of the following financial sites to help with the analysis: "Morningstar," "StockAnalysis," "MarketWatch," or "Yahoo Finance." These sites will list the companies under their stock symbols, so they need to perform a quick search to check the stock symbol and name they trade under on the stock market. Aspects they may want to look at include:

- Earnings per share (EPS): This measures a company's profitability. It tells you how much profit the company makes for each outstanding share of common stock.

  ○ What to look for: Consistent growth over time is a great indication that the company is performing well.

- Price-to-earnings (P/E) ratio: This ratio indicates the price of shares relative to the company's EPS. Investors look at this to determine the relative value of the stocks.

  ○ What to look for: A ratio of between 15 and 20 is average. If you're investing in growth stocks, the ratio could be on the higher end, while value stocks will have a lower-end ratio.

- Dividend Yield: This is also a ratio that reveals how much the company pays out each year in dividends relative to the price of their stocks.
  - What to look for: A classic yield is between 2 and 4%. Although a higher yield can be tempting, one should proceed with caution.

- When evaluating these metrics, it's essential to consider them in the context of the industry, the company's growth prospects, and overall market conditions. Always use multiple financial metrics and qualitative factors for a comprehensive analysis.

Step 6: There are sites where you and your teen can create mock portfolios and take their knowledge for a test drive before committing to the real thing. They can compete with their friends or family and build up experience without losing any money.

Some of the dummy online trading portfolios I know include "HowTheMarketWorks," "MockPortfolios," "Wall Street Survivor," and "MarketWatch Virtual Stock Exchange."

Step 7: When your teen is ready, you can look at opening a custodial brokerage account for them. If they're not old enough yet, you will need to do it for them. Reassure your teen that they will still own all the assets even though you opened the account. You will be in charge of the account and all investments, though. No changes can be made without your input or consent. Once they are old enough, they can take over the account.

There are three main factors to consider when choosing an online custodial brokerage account for your teen:

- **Fractional shares:** If your teen doesn't earn a lot of money, chances are they may not invest a large amount. If their intention is to invest in reputable companies that have high stock prices, they need to find a custodial account where they can buy fractional shares.

- **Free trading:** Some brokerages may even offer free trading, i.e., no charge when buying and selling stocks. A zero transaction fee is ideal, especially for teens where their investments may not be as large yet.

- **Low minimum balance requirement:** Most online brokerages have a minimum balance requirement; however, there are certain accounts where this is $0.

Some of the teen-friendly broker accounts include Bloom, Interactive Brokers, Greenlightcard, Charles Schwab, Acorns, Stockpile, and Ally Invest.

Diverse Portfolio

We briefly touched on this, but in a nutshell, diversifying your portfolio means that you don't put all your eggs in one basket. Diversifying may mean having different types of assets, investing in different stocks, or a combination of both.

An easy way to explain diversification to your teen is to use a sweet shop as an example. If they only like one type of sweet and the store runs out, they might feel a little sad and leave the store empty-handed. However, if they like different types of sweets and the store runs out of one, they have many others to choose from. This is what diversification does—if one investment performs poorly, the main investment portfolio may not be as affected, especially if the others are doing well.

Some people struggle to determine where exactly their investments should go to diversify their portfolio between stocks and bonds. Allocation can depend on several factors, but you could use the simple equation of subtracting your (or your teen's) current age from 100. That's a good indication of how much of the investments should be in stocks, with the remainder in bonds. If your teen is 15, they should have around 85% of their investment in stocks and 15% in bonds. The younger you are, the more risk you can afford. As you grow older, it's important to adapt the portfolio accordingly.

Using the buy-and-hold strategy is another great way to ensure consistent growth and reduce the pressure of always looking for the next best thing. There is nothing wrong with buying stocks and holding on to them, regardless of the fluctuations in the market. In some instances, it may make sense to sell the stock if it reaches its full potential early in the investment or there is a threat that the stock will crash and burn, but in general, the buy-and-hold strategy is great for those who are still learning the ropes.

You can use the board game Monopoly again to teach them about diversification. By playing the game, your teen will have exposure to:

- **Asset allocation:** With Monopoly, you learn how to balance buying additional properties, adding houses, or replacing houses with hotels. This helps you learn how to invest across all assets you own and the impact this has instead of focusing on only one.

- **Liquidity:** When there is an emergency, and you need cash, you can sell some properties or assets to gain access to quick cash. This simulates selling investments in the event of an emergency.

- **Planning for the future:** In Monopoly, you don't have unlimited access to everything. You need to carefully decide which properties and assets to invest in with the available money you have in order to ensure that you are in the best financial position. The more diverse the portfolio is, the more sustainable the investments will be.

- **Risk management:** Knowing how to balance the purchasing of properties, houses, and hotels versus paying taxes on those properties is a risk. Whenever you roll the dice and land on Chance, there is a possibility that you may need to pay money to the bank or even move to one of your opponents' properties and pay them rent. With every roll of the dice, there is a risk. Deciding whether to save money or invest is a risk management technique.

Cryptocurrencies

This is a concept that has been around for a while, but very few people know much about it. Although cryptocurrencies can be a good investment, you shouldn't encourage your teen to invest in them right now. Let them build up some experience and get a feel for trading before they step into the cryptocurrency world. This market is very volatile, which means it comes at a high risk, and the reward is not always worth it.

The most well-known cryptocurrency is Bitcoin, with Ethereum in a close second. Regardless of how popular Bitcoin is, it suffered a massive knock in value from November 2021 to June 2022, declining in value by an astonishing 70% (Modu, 2024). Although cryptocurrencies go through cycles and regain value in the process, they are volatile assets that are not suitable for beginner investors.

ACTIVITY

We've covered the basics; now it's time for you to create an action plan to help your teen with their first investment. The action plan doesn't have to be intricate, and you can add to it as you go along, but it should at least cover these topics:

- Help them with the steps to open a checking account if they don't already have one. They will need to provide certain documentation, such as a valid ID, proof of address, and your ID (if they are still minors). Most major banks offer bank accounts specially designed for teens where the bank and transaction fees are low. Do some research to ensure you get the best deal.

- Explore additional apps and online resources that deal with investing. You can use the contents of this chapter to review the references. There are many online resources and apps that provide an overview and details of the process of investing and what to look for.

- You need to help your teen understand how investing works. Once you've gone through the concepts, ask them to explain to you what they understand. This way, you can fill in any gaps and supplement their knowledge if their understanding is on point.

- Make sure that you use their savings or pocket money to invest so that they feel responsible for the investments. If you use your own money, they might not pay as much attention and forget about it in a few days or weeks.

- Have regular check-ins with your teen to monitor the performance of their investments. Ask whether they would like to make any changes and discuss why you agree or disagree. This cultivates healthy investing habits that they will foster well into adulthood.

Investing is one of the most complex topics that you need to cover with your teen, so if they don't seem too interested at first, don't worry and don't give up hope. Talk to them about it every chance you get. Start small with simple concepts and games to pique their interest before introducing them to the stock market.

SUMMARY

- When investing, there should be a long-term focus and not a need for immediate gratification. It's not the most exciting thing at the moment, but it holds long-term benefits.

- Getting your teen invested from a young age has many benefits, including cultivating healthy financial habits, taking advantage of compound interest, and being able to take higher risks due to low expenses and available years to recover.

- Teens may not be able to set up their own accounts for investing and need an adult to help them. They will still own the investments; however, the adult will have full control of the investments until the teen is of legal age.

- Giving your teen the tools and knowledge they need to invest successfully is the key to becoming an expert later.

- Explain the concept of diversification and how this reduces the risk of losing.

One thing that may play a role in their interest (or lack thereof) in investing is their emotions. In Chapter 7, we will look at how emotions can affect a teen's spending and investing habits and how you can help them manage these emotions.

Chapter 7

Eliminating Emotional Influences From Financial Decisions

> *"Only when you combine sound intellect with emotional discipline do you get rational behavior."*
> — **Warren Buffett**

E motions are powerful. They can control all our decisions and, ultimately, our lives. Although they are an important part of being human, we shouldn't allow our emotions to overcome us and start controlling every part of our lives.

Even as adults, we sometimes make decisions (even financial ones) based on how we feel. Imagine how tough it must be for teens! In addition to being in limbo between a child and an adult, they are still discovering themselves, trying to find out what they like and what career they want to pursue one day, all while trying to ride the rollercoaster of emotions without making mistakes that may have an impact on their future.

The thing is, our emotions change constantly. Making investment and money decisions based on our emotional state is dangerous because these decisions are not based on facts. As soon as our emotions change, we might regret our initial decision and want to change our mind.

Knowing how to handle emotions and keep emotions out of financial decisions is a superpower that will benefit your teen for years to come.

Emotional Investing

You'd be surprised at how many people make emotional investment decisions. This is when you decide to buy or sell investments based on your feelings instead of the facts. We often make the mistake of investing in something that seems successful, either due to word of mouth or out of fear for the future, without properly assessing the financials of the investments. Greed and anxiety are other examples of such feelings.

When investing, we should be level-headed. We shouldn't have any preconceived ideas of what may or may not happen. We should expect risk and hope for reward based on research done beforehand.

Emotional investing is common among younger people, especially as they are just starting to grasp the potential and risks of investing. In haste, they end up investing in the "next best thing" without really looking into it.

Stages of Emotional Investing

Understanding the why behind it makes it easier to explain and avoid it. There are different stages of emotional investing that capture the reasons why we are susceptible to emotional investing really well. It occurs in a cycle, starting with optimism; it leads to anxiety, then panic, and then just as we start losing hope, things pick up, and we're back at optimism. This is all due to the way the stock market operates and the fluctuations in value. This causes fluctuations in our emotions when we use emotions to invest.

- **Optimism:** This is when someone is just starting out and remembers all the good things everyone was telling them about the stock they've purchased. The value is growing in an upward trend, and the person can see what a difference it is going to make in the future. They start tracking their money goals and get ready to start ticking them off.

- **Anxiety:** As soon as the value drops slightly, they may start experiencing anxiety. They're not sure whether they should be holding or selling. What if it drops more, and they lose everything? But what if this is just a small dip, and after this, it will improve significantly?

- **Panic:** If the downward trend doesn't stop, they go into panic mode, and this is where most people end up selling. Although they have lost money, they are concerned about losing even more and would rather accept the small loss and try to recover than lose everything.

- **Losing hope:** Just as things start to spiral out of control, the market changes and stocks go back up. The ones who didn't sell are happy and move back into optimism, while those who sold have lost hope in that specific investment and are either looking for other options or considering reinvesting as the value continues to grow.

Those with advanced knowledge in investing understand the bull and bear markets and expect these fluctuations based on the historical data of their investment. They don't allow these fluctuations to force them into making emotional decisions but rely on the facts to drive their decision-making.

The two emotions that drive emotional investing are fear and greed. Experts say that fear and greed can cause people to ignore self-control and common sense and pursue something despite warning signs. They are both key drivers in humans when it comes to money.

Possible Pitfalls During the Planning Stage of Investing

New investors might run into the below pitfalls while they are creating their investment profile. Although it applies to investing, these pitfalls are all related to emotional investing and should be explained to your teen.

- **Anchoring bias:** This happens when an investor anchors their entire strategy on the first bit of information they receive either online or through trusted individuals, which leads to them not doing any research of their own and missing potential opportunities.

- **Familiarity bias:** With this bias, an investor remains focused on the brands and markets that they know well and invests in those instead of assets that are more suited for their risk profile.

- **Herd mentality:** Herd mentality means that an investor follows what everyone else is doing instead of exploring assets that will benefit them and work well in their portfolio.

- **Restraint bias:** An investor thinks that they will be able to face temptation when the market fluctuates and, as a result, have no contingencies in place; however, when the heat is turned up, they fall into the cycle of emotional investing.

Possible Pitfalls During the Investing Stage

There are also certain pitfalls to look out for during the investing stage when they've already started building their portfolio.

- **Win-loss ratio:** Everyone makes bad decisions sometimes and needs to cut losses when that happens. However, in some instances, the investor insists that every transaction they make should be successful. This means that instead of cutting their losses when they've made a mistake, they end up holding on to the bad investment.

- **Loss aversion bias:** Nobody likes losing, but with investing, the risk is always there. An investor with a loss aversion bias chooses investments with a lower risk because they are scared of losing and, as a result, make little to no gains on their investments. Although this is very safe, it's not the ideal risk profile, especially for a teen or young adult. Risk is necessary but should be carefully calculated and considered.

- **Confirmation bias:** This is when an investor makes a decision and, instead of taking new information into account, they look for anything that can support their initial decision. Although the initial decision may have been the right one at the time, one should always take new research and information into account and make adjustments where necessary.

Avoid Emotional Investing

Explain the four stages of emotional investing with your teen and make sure they understand the concept. If they can understand and recognize it, they will be in a better position to avoid it or get out of it before it's too late. Ask them to engage with you before making any hasty decisions regarding their investments and chat through it with them.

Share the tips below with them to avoid emotional investing.

Don't Try to Time the Market

Some people try to find the perfect time to invest by attempting to predict when the market will rise and fall. Even the most seasoned investors have difficulty timing the market correctly.

The best thing your teen can do is to get into it. Start today or whenever they decide to embark on their investment journey. They shouldn't wait for the value to drop and then hope that it picks up again.

Focus on Business Performance and Not Stock Performance

Making decisions on stock performance is part of emotional investing. Stock performance is not an accurate representation of whether the investment was a good or bad idea.

The key thing to focus on is the business performance, i.e., how well the business for the investment is performing. The stocks will fluctuate based on whether they are in a bull or bear market, but the value over time is determined by the business performance.

Create Diversity in Their Investment Portfolio

We've touched on diversifying their portfolio a few times. It will definitely help to avoid emotional investing since a drop in the value of one asset will have a small effect on a properly diverse portfolio. In fact, the drop in value may even be absorbed and overpowered by another asset that is performing well.

Don't Look at Daily Progress

There is nothing worse than constantly checking investments and seeing every small change that is occurring. Depending on the volatility, a single stock can go through so many changes in a single day that one might end up selling and buying the same stock multiple times a day.

Advise your teen not to track their investment progress every day, as this might create some anxiety and panic when there are minor fluctuations. Checking every few days or once a week (depending on the volatility of the stock) is more than enough.

Look at the Bigger Picture

Encourage your teen to look at the bigger picture when they feel like they want to make an investment decision based on emotion. Going back to the initial reason for investing is a good starting point. They can use the below questions to bring the bigger picture back into their line of vision.

- Does their portfolio include enough diversity to cushion any blows?
- Has their financial situation changed since they started investing?
- Are they still chasing their initial investment goals, or have these changed?
- Are they taking the appropriate amount of risk?

Consider Dollar-Cost Averaging

This concept was touched on earlier in the chapter and is an excellent way to sidestep emotional investing. It works on the basis of investing a specific amount into the same asset at regular intervals, regardless of the current value or fluctuations in the market.

Let's look at a quick example of what this might look like. This is just an example and not based on a real stock, but it illustrates the concept well.

If your teen chooses Stock A and decides to invest $15 each month for a year, their investment might look a little something like this:

Month	Investment (a)	Price per unit (b)	Total Units Bought (a/b)
1	$15	$2.50	6
2	$15	$ 3.50	4.29
3	$15	$3.00	5
4	$15	$2.50	6
5	$15	$2.00	7.5
6	$15	$1.50	10
7	$15	$2.00	7.5
8	$15	$2.50	6
9	$15	$2.50	6
10	$15	$2.00	7.5
11	$15	$1.50	10
12	$15	$1.50	10
Total	$180	$2.25	85.79

If they had initially invested the entire $180, they would have only been able to purchase 72 units, whereas, with dollar-cost averaging (DCA), they have now purchased 85.79 units with the same amount of money, ignoring the fluctuations in the market. Of course, this may not always be the case, and the best price may have been in month one or two, but this is impossible to know upfront. DCA is a strategy used and loved by many investors.

Seek Professional Advice

A financial advisor is in the best position to help with financial decisions. If neither you nor your teen are sure whether they are making the right decision, consider consulting with a financial advisor with experience in the market.

Signs to Look Out For

Your teen might not immediately realize that they are allowing their emotions to control their investment decisions, which is why you need to know what to look out for to steer them back on the right path. You need to engage with your teen regularly and discuss their investments and investment habits to know what is going on.

For each of the below, I have included a question you can ask your teen to gain a better understanding of where their head is at and identify whether they need additional support from you.

They Forget the Basics

We've covered the fundamental investment principles in this chapter that they should always keep in mind when investing, such as common pitfalls, doing your research, diversifying your portfolio, taking risks you can afford, not being afraid to take risks, etc.

Forgetting these basics can be another mistake new investors, especially teens, make because they get sucked into the opinions of others or existing biases toward brands and companies.

You can monitor this by asking them the following questions and analyzing their answer:

- Do you make any investments based on what your friends say, how popular a brand or company is, or what you read on social media?

Their response will indicate whether they remember and apply the fundamentals. You may want to go over the basics once more and clarify the potential pitfalls of basing investment decisions on the opinions of others.

Trading Too Much

This could be a problem when they constantly buy and sell their investments in the hopes of finding better deals. It's not a very good investment strategy, and they're not really learning anything from the process.

Hopping from one good thing to another without allowing investments to settle and grow may lead to stagnation, meaning that although they may spend a lot of time in the market, they have nothing to show for it.

Monitor this by asking them the following question:

- How often do you find yourself trading assets, hoping to get better returns on your investment?

Depending on their answer, try to find out what they base their decisions on when they do trade and ensure this is good investment practice.

They React to Short-Term Fluctuations in the Market

As soon as there is the smallest dip in the market, they sell their investment immediately without analyzing the stock or market or doing any further research. This is especially the case if the asset has been on an upward trend for a while and suddenly experiences a minor fluctuation. They are so scared they will lose the gains they've made and jump ship.

This could be the right thing to do, or it may be a mistake. Most assets bounce back again, especially if they've been around for a while and have good financial indicators overall. However, people who react to these short-term fluctuations never look at the financial indicators.

One way you can monitor this is by regularly asking the following question:

- Do you become anxious and consider selling your investments when you observe any market changes?

If they simply answer "yes," you need to discuss this with them and reemphasize the steps they can take to prevent their emotions from controlling their decisions. If, however, the answer is "Yes, but..." or anything else, this can spark a great conversation between you two regarding their thoughts and will provide you with insights into how they're managing their investments.

Putting All Their Eggs in One Basket

Sometimes, an asset may perform really well, and your teen may be tempted to put all their money into that one investment. They may have heard a success story from someone else or read about someone online, and it sounded like a good idea, especially if they knew which asset the person invested in.

Anyone can fall into this trap when we take our eyes off the goal. Investing is not primarily about earning money quickly. Real and proper investing takes time and patience. A get-rich-quick asset screams bad news and should be an immediate red flag for your teen.

You can check in on this by asking them the following questions:

- What does your investment portfolio look like at the moment?

- Have you been tempted to move everything over to a single asset in the hopes that you will make millions from it?

Asking these questions will help you identify whether you need to discuss diversification with your teen and whether they understand the concept of investing.

Following the Crowd
The danger with this is that they end up not making the right investment decisions for their risk profile, which may lead to disappointment down the line. Buying or selling certain assets because everyone else is doing it is not sound investing. If your teen has fallen victim to this, you need to have a discussion with them regarding the dangers of following the crowd and what to do instead—make investment decisions based on the facts. Help them to review the performance of the asset and business before they make these decisions.

If they haven't confided in you about this yet, you can ask the following question to monitor it:

- If one of your friends had to come to you and tell you that they have the best deal for you to double your money in a few months, would you consider it?

Their answer will tell you everything you need to know. If they hastily answer without thinking about it, they are at risk of falling into this trap. In this case, you may need to discuss why this is a bad idea and what they should consider or look out for before accepting the deal. However, if they give it some thought and tell you that it depends on a few factors, get ready for a fruitful discussion.

EMOTIONAL SPENDING

Emotional spending is a lot like emotional investing; however, instead of being restricted to investing, it actually extends to everything else. Our emotions can cause us to buy things on impulse or recklessly spend money on things that were never in the budget.

Some people spend money when they feel sad or depressed because buying things makes them feel better. Others may spend money when they're very happy and want to make everyone around them happy too. Whether you are driven by good or bad emotions, emotional spending leads to unnecessary purchases and affects your cash flow for the necessary expenses.

Emotional spending can get us into a lot of trouble. If you don't address and curb this while your teen is young, they may have difficulties managing money when they're well into their adult lives.

Causes

Emotional spending, or impulse buying, can be caused by several factors, such as:

- **Being impulsive:** Impulsivity might be part of your teen's character. Being impulsive means that you do something without thinking or worrying about the possible consequences. Although adults are also impulsive, this is more common among kids and teens because their brains are still developing.

- **Current emotional state:** As they grow into young adults, teens may experience a wave of emotions daily. They are more likely to spend money when they are feeling sad, anxious, or bad about themselves. They purchase items they believe will bring them happiness and resolve their current situation.

- **For sensation:** Experiencing something new is a lot more exciting for teens than adults. If they have the opportunity to buy something new and exciting that they've been searching for, the chances of them making the purchase are quite high.

- **Marketing tactics:** Companies pay marketers a lot of money to influence people to purchase their products. By using limited-time offers teens can't resist, attractive packaging, and catchy slogans, they convince teens to give in to impulse buying.

- **Peer pressure:** Where friends are involved, there is always additional pressure to have what they have. Teens are more susceptible than adults to peer pressure and may give in to impulse buying to fit in.

When It Becomes an Issue

We all give in to some retail therapy every now and then. It's not always bad, but it can become an issue. Those who continuously give in to emotional spending can develop a psychological disorder called compulsive buying.

This disorder is characterized by impulsive buying of unnecessary things, regardless of emotional state. The person is unable to control their impulses and obsessively buys things they want without thinking about the consequences.

Money Personality Types

In this book, we will concentrate on three money personality types: compulsive spender, compulsive saver, and saver-splurger. These are the most common money personality types among people, including teens.

By being able to categorize your teen into one of the personality types, you will know what to look out for and how to help them be smarter with their money. Go through the common pitfalls and ways to overcome them with your teen.

Compulsive Spender

A compulsive spender loves to spend their money any chance they get. They enjoy treating those around them to something, anything, for no particular reason. They give in to immediate gratification, especially when they're feeling emotional, and spend money on unnecessary purchases without remorse.

Compulsive spenders tend to never stop. They end up in large amounts of debt and, even then, will take any opportunity to spend money. They will actively seek reasons to spend money, such as a sale, and purchase items that were never even on their radar simply because they are discounted. Most of the time, they spend more than they earn and have a hard time getting out of their bad financial situation.

Help compulsive spenders by encouraging them to create and follow a budget. Help them to track their expenses, including any compulsive buys, and show them what a difference cutting out compulsive spending would make. This doesn't mean that they can't have money allocated towards spending, but that it should happen in moderation. Build a spending category into their budget so they don't feel like you've removed all their fun.

Compulsive Saver

This is the complete opposite of a compulsive spender. They tend to save money without having an end goal in mind because they are afraid that they will run out of savings. They believe this will make them feel more secure, but no amount of money ever seems to be enough. When they do need to spend money, they look for the cheapest option to spend as little as possible.

Having too much savings or being too prepared, can you ever say it's a bad idea? And the answer is no, however, a compulsive saver is so focused and worried about tomorrow that they forget to live today. They never get to enjoy the money they work so hard making.

You can support a compulsive saver by helping them find a balance. It's all about moderation. Saving for the future is important and should be prioritized, but it's also important for them to enjoy their lives now. It's okay to get a cup of coffee, buy that new shirt, or watch a movie with friends. As long as these activities are kept in moderation, they will still save more than enough.

Saver-Splurger

This is a combination of the above two personality types. They are good at saving up quite a bit, but then a shopping spree impulse comes out of nowhere, and they splurge on unnecessary items. Most of the time, they would use the savings they have and rarely have something to show for it. They just had the urge to spend their money on something.

Unlike compulsive spenders, saver-splurgers feel disappointed in themselves when they end up pushing the savings they worked so hard to save into something that they don't really need. Going from excessive saving to excessive spending has an exhausting effect on our emotions and can leave these individuals stressed and drained.

You can support a saver-splurger by asking them to let you know when they feel the need to spend their money on something. You can keep them accountable. You don't have to tell them that the purchase is a bad idea, but you should try using probing questions to get them to think rationally about the situation. Remind them of the financial goals they've set for themselves and how this purchase will affect their goals.

ACTIVITY

This activity will help your teen to keep track of and reflect on their emotional spending level. Copy the below worksheets and give them to your teen to complete. Your teen might not be super into this activity, so it might help if you complete it with them. You can make it a fun, interactive activity where you discuss their emotions while spending money and chat about some examples. Share your own experiences to show them that they're not alone.

Worksheet 1

The first worksheet is to understand where their current mindset is and when they are most likely to spend money.

Emotion	Likelihood to spend (Scale from 1–10)
Angry	
Sad	
Guilty	
Jealous	
Stressed	
Overwhelmed	
Happy	
Generous	

Where your teen has identified they have a higher chance of spending, engage in a discussion with them to get to the root of the problem. Perhaps they tend to spend more money when they are feeling generous because they enjoy the feeling of others appreciating them. Ask them what result the purchase has—what emotion they feel just after they've spent the money. This will create a great foundation for a discussion about how their emotions influence their money habits and why it's important to get a hold of it now before it gets out of hand.

Worksheet 2

The second worksheet is to keep track of any emotional spending during the week. Once the week is over, go through the worksheet with them and help them reflect on why they felt the purchase was necessary and whether it made them feel better.

If they can pinpoint when they spend the most money, they can start being more vigilant when they feel that way and choose to replace a shopping spree with something else that will make them feel better.

I have completed the first line as an example. Instead of using one week, you can extend it to a month (i.e., track weekly purchases). It depends on how often your teen gives in to the impulse of buying. You may not have any incidents in a week but a few later in the month, especially right after they receive their money.

Day	Purchase	Ammount	Emotion
Monday	Coffee at Starbucks	$2.95	Happy
Tuesday			
Wednesday			
Thursday			
Friday			
Saturday			
Sunday			

Helping your teen get a handle on emotional investing and spending will improve their financial habits and support a great foundation into adulthood. The less they allow their emotions to control them, the more they will be able to save and put towards retirement.

Summary

- Emotional investing is when we make investing decisions based on our immediate emotions instead of looking at the facts.
  - The stages of emotional investing are optimism, anxiety, panic, and losing hope.
  - Common pitfalls experienced by new investors, like your teen, include:
    - Anchoring bias
    - Familiarity bias
    - Herd mentality
    - Restraint bias
    - Win-loss ratio
    - Loss aversion bias
    - Confirmation bias
  - Help to avoid emotional investing by just getting into the market instead of trying to time it, focusing on the business performance, diversifying their portfolio, not checking their investments daily, using the dollar-cost averaging strategy, and seeking professional advice.
- Emotional spending is when you buy something based on your emotions because you think it will make you feel better.
  - You can help your teen manage emotional spending by creating and sticking to a budget, tracking and re-

flecting on their spending habits, and understanding their underlying emotional triggers.

The last chapter deals with the importance of encouraging your teen to plan for retirement from an early age with strategies to achieve their retirement goals.

Chapter 8

Retiring Rich by Planning and Taking Action Early

"The question isn't at what age I want to retire, it's at what income."

— George Foreman —

I love this quote by George Foreman. Everyone is always so focused on the age of retirement, but what we should actually be focused on is the income we want once we retire. If your teen doesn't plan properly and decides to retire too early, their retirement funds may run out within a few years, leaving them with no income in their elderly days.

I know many people who wish they had started planning and saving for retirement at a younger age, but no one ever regrets starting too early. The sooner you start, the better.

A common mistake teens make when it comes to retirement planning is to think that it's too early to even think about it. They spend their prime years when they have little to no responsibilities, spending their money on other things and forgetting to include retirement planning in their budget.

LOOKING TO THE FUTURE

This is where you, as their parent, can make a difference. Have these conversations with them early and explain the importance and benefits of starting while they're young. Okay, it might not be a very exciting topic for your teen to chat about at the moment, but if you can paint them a picture of an amazing retirement, they might pay attention to what you have to say.

Ask them to think about what they imagine retirement might be like. If they have grandparents who are retired, they may use their lives as an example. If their grandparents planned and saved for retirement properly, you may not need to do as much work from your end. However, if their grandparents currently live in a small apartment or share a home with them due to financial constraints, struggle to make ends meet each month, and frequently express concerns about money, it's important to understand that this is their frame of reference. This may explain why they aren't very enthusiastic about retirement.

Regardless of which bucket they fall into, you can still help them to picture a better retirement. They'll be able to do whatever they want: Travel the world, have a vacation home close to the coast or in different countries, have a paid-off house and car, and so much more. The sky is the limit.

Whatever they want to achieve by the time they retire should be part of their retirement plan, including a retirement fund that can fund all these dreams. Remind them of the power of compound interest and do a simple calculation to show them what a difference it will make if they start now, even if it's with a small amount.

College Versus Retirement

Should your teen be saving for college or retirement?

The answer is not as easy as you would like it to be. There are several factors to consider when deciding on this; however, the important thing is that they invest and save. If you can get them to start investing and saving for the future, that is already a step further than some other teens.

Ideally, they should save or invest in both. Before we continue with this important piece, make sure your teen understands the difference between saving and investing. Savings accounts typically generate minimal interest and are commonly used to save money for specific goals, like making a purchase or funding education. Investing is for a longer period with the aim of getting out much more than what you put in. We've dealt with both of these concepts in earlier chapters.

Saving is more related to college, while investing focuses more on retirement. Depending on your financial situation and your teen's financial and life goals, they may choose to save and invest for different reasons. Ideally, they should do both.

College Savings Fund

There are specific savings accounts that your teen can open that are dedicated to education.

You get two different types of 529 plans: a 529 prepaid tuition plan and a 529 savings plan. Your teen doesn't need both, but it is helpful to know the difference between the two to make the right decision.

The 529 savings plan is available in most states, but the fees and interest rates may vary. When choosing a 529 savings plan, the savings are invested in mutual funds, ETFs, and bond funds, similar to a 401K and IRA retirement plan. Anyone can contribute to this fund for your teen, so they can even add this to their birthday and Christmas wish lists. The more contributions they receive into the savings account, the more they can put toward their retirement.

The 529 prepaid tuition plan gives families the opportunity to pay tuition fees in advance based on the current fees. This is not available in every state and is not an investment like the 529 savings plan but rather an option to start paying tuition now to reduce the costs later.

By starting a 529 plan, they can avoid applying for a loan or be able to reduce the loan by a significant amount. Some students take years to pay off their student loans. This is a large stressor they can avoid in their adult life.

Retirement

According to Dickler (2024), up to 83% of teens aged 13 to 18 have retirement in mind. The problem is that most of them believe they should be saving for their retirement in a normal savings account. Although that's better than not saving at all, the best strategy is to use investments to start growing your money for retirement, as this will yield a greater return on investment and can take your retirement from average to amazing.

HELP THEM PLAN FOR RETIREMENT

Based on research, we can see that many teens have started thinking about retirement, but they're not sure what the next steps are. Set your teen on the right path by sharing these tips with them.

- **Start as soon as possible:** The earlier they start planning and saving for retirement, the more financially secure they will be once they get there.

- **Information is key:** They need to be educated about the different retirement plans and what they can invest in now. Some companies also offer a contribution towards a retirement plan (401K), but there is no need for them to wait for employment to start saving.

- **401(k):** At the moment, your teen might not need too much information on this. Some companies offer a 401(k) where they match the contribution made by the employee or a percentage thereof. If your teen gets the opportunity to do this, they should take advantage of it. The additional amount contributed by the employer makes a huge difference in the long run.

- **Goal setting:** This is where they decide what they want to do once they retire. How do they plan on spending their days? What income do they aim to have at retirement? Do they want a house in the Maldives or a few investments across the globe? These are all important and realistic goals that they can set for themselves. Encourage them to think big and not limit themselves based on what they think is possible. Goal setting is discussed in more detail in the activity section of this chapter. They may not have a good idea of what their life could look like in a few years from now. It's important for you to share some examples here of either your life or someone they might know so that they have a reference point from which to work.

- **Adjust the budget:** Once you've had the discussion about retirement, revisit their budget with them and incorporate their retirement savings into it. Use the goals they set above and remind them to revise their goals and budget regularly as their situation changes.

- **Be aggressive:** We discussed investments in detail in the previous chapter. The younger you are, the bigger your appetite for risk should be and the more aggressive you can be with your investments. This does not mean that your teen should be reckless and choose the most aggressive, most volatile investments. But they shouldn't be afraid to take risks.

- **For emergencies:** Educate them on having an emergency fund to cover their expenses in case of an emergency. This could be anything from a health issue to an accident. By creating this fund, they can use it when needed instead of needing to cash out their retirement savings (which can become tempting when they need the money).

  - When creating their emergency fund, help them to make a list of expenses that will qualify as an emergency. Without this clear list, anything could feel like an emergency (like not having anything to wear to Saturday's party).

  - The ideal emergency fund should be able to cover at least five to six months of the essential expenses. Since your teen doesn't have a lot of essential expenses at the moment, it doesn't have to be a large amount right now. Explain the premise of an emergency fund and how much they should try to build one so they can adjust it as their financial situation and responsibilities change. They can't keep the same emergency fund in their 30s that they had in their teens!

- **Open a Roth IRA:** A Roth IRA is a very versatile investment and can be saved for retirement, withdrawn money for a down payment on a house, or even used to fund college. This may be quite tempting to take advantage of, which is why a college fund and emergency savings are important—to prevent unnecessary withdrawals and ensure that your teen maximizes the power of compound interest.

  - They can only contribute income received from an employer to the Roth IRA account, so no extra pocket money or birthday money can be deposited.

  - There is a maximum annual contribution, which changes every year. Make sure your teen is aware of the limit to avoid disappointment later.

  - At the age of 59 and a half, the withdrawal becomes tax-free, provided that the Roth IRA has been open for at least five years. They are able to make withdrawals before this; however, any withdrawals on earnings will attract penalties and be subject to tax.

ACTIVITY

The final activity of this book is to help your teen set some financial goals. Setting goals should be a part of every aspect of their lives, which means that you should teach them how to do it. Setting a goal is one thing; setting an achievable goal is something entirely different.

A methodology I like to use when setting goals is SMART. A SMART goal is:

- Specific: There is no room for confusion or interpretation. It's not broad, and there are no grey areas. The goal is clear and specific.

- Measurable: Being able to measure progress is a vital part of goal setting. If you can't measure the goal and progress made, how will you know if you have achieved it?

- Achievable: The goal should be something that is possible, given their age, income, or dreams. If it's a retirement goal, it doesn't have to be achievable in the near future but should be by the time they retire.

- Realistic: Being realistic means that they can reach the goal. For example, the goal can't be to save $500 by the end of the year if they can only contribute $10 a month.

- Time-bound: With no time stamp to it, a goal can be ongoing forever, and they might lose interest in chasing it down.

Let's look at a quick example. Let's say they set a goal like:

I want to save money.

Although that goal is great and definitely something they should aspire to do, it doesn't meet any of the requirements to be a SMART goal. Let's change it up a bit.

I want to save $500 to buy the new PlayStation in 12 months. I will do this by contributing $45 a month towards it.

This goal can be SMART. Let's break it down.

- **Specific:** It is a specific goal because it states that they want to save money to buy a PlayStation.

- **Measurable:** This goal is easy to measure because the end goal is to save $500, so tracking progress and knowing when they have achieved it is possible.

- **Achievable:** If they save $45 a month for 12 months, they will have $540. This is enough to buy the new PlayStation.

- **Realistic:** We'll assume that they earn $170 a month, which means they are capable of contributing $45 toward this goal.

- **Time-bound:** The goal includes a time frame of 12 months.

Using the SMART method and example provided, encourage your teen to set some SMART financial goals of their own. It can be for their retirement or just goals in general.

When setting these goals, use real-life examples to give them a general idea of the types of goals they can set for themselves. If you can, share some of the goals that you've set in the past and achieved. You can inspire them by sharing your success story and the challenges you may have faced in chasing after your goals.

Achieving a goal should be a big deal. Keep them motivated by celebrating with them, regardless of how small the victory might seem. You can even help them break their medium- and long-term goals into smaller steps and celebrate every small win. This will help to keep them motivated and encourage them to set new goals once they have achieved the existing ones.

Summary

- Your teen should not focus on the age at which they want to retire but on the income they want to get once they retire.

- It's never too early to help your teen prepare for retirement. The sooner they get started, the more benefit they will derive from it. The earlier they start, the more they can take advantage of compound investment.

- To help your teen start planning, prompt them to visualize what they want their retirement to look like. Share extravagant ideas to ensure they're not limiting their thinking.

- There is a difference between saving for something short-term and investing long-term. Savings can be made for college and small items, while investments can be made for retirement and larger purchases.

- Setting SMART financial goals is key to achieving success.

Empowering the
Next Generation Together

*"Education is the most powerful weapon
which you can use to change the world."*

Nelson Mandela

"How do I teach my teen about money?" This is a question many parents ask as they realize how essential financial literacy is in shaping their child's future. We often reflect on the financial lessons we wish we had learned earlier.

Teaching teenagers about money involves more than just teaching them how to save or invest; it's about cultivating the mindset, habits, and skills needed for making wise financial choices throughout their lives.

Financial independence, stability, and success are built upon a solid foundation of financial literacy. I wrote this book to give parents some tools that can make things a bit easier - tools that most of our parents never got when we were kids.

But here's the catch: a book can't make a difference without reaching the right people. That's why I'm asking you to join me on this journey. If you find this guide helpful and believe it can benefit other parents and their teenagers, please consider leaving an honest review. By sharing your feedback, you can help other parents discover this resource and empower their children with essential financial skills for adulthood.

Together, we can help to create a generation of financially confident young adults.

Conclusion

Your teen should be financially literate if you want them to be successful and financially independent. As parents, you need to ensure that they understand the basics of finances and the importance of making sound financial decisions.

By openly engaging with them about money and using practical lessons, you can empower them to handle any possible financial hurdles with ease in adulthood. Cultivating healthy habits from a young age will help them avoid common pitfalls that may lead to financial struggles later in life.

From a young age, a lot of us were taught that money is a taboo subject to discuss, even among family members. I believe this is why so many people are struggling to make ends meet and adopt healthy money habits. By not discussing money and successes and failures, we deprive others of learning from our mistakes and set them up for failure until they can find their own secret recipe to success. Although some may find this recipe early in life, for others, it takes years.

It's our job to set our teens up for success. We shouldn't let them try and fail because that's how we learned. Yes, they need to make their own mistakes, too, but we can help them prevent catastrophes and build a good foundation now.

Using the P.R.O.S.P.E.R. approach will help you package the information in a manner that is easily digestible for your teen and properly structured to ensure all aspects are covered.

- **P**lanning with a budget is essential to success.

- o Help your teen learn how to budget and include savings in their budget.

- o A budget should make provisions for income, expenses (fixed and variable), investments and savings, and debt repayment.

- o As they progress through the month, it's important to track their expenses. This will make it easier to identify unnecessary expenses and optimize their budget next time.

- **R**ecognizing what compound interest is and knowing how to take advantage of it is key to growing their nest egg. The sooner they understand and use compound interest, the more they will benefit from it.

  - o The sooner they start saving and investing, the more compound interest they will receive. Making regular contributions and reinvesting any payouts are great ways to make compound interest work for you.

  - o Compound interest can also be bad, like in the case of personal loans and credit cards. A large balance will accumulate large compound interest that needs to be paid back, which means it takes longer to settle the debt.

- **O**vercoming debt and the stress that goes along with it is a key pillar for living in financial freedom. Nobody likes to have debt that weighs them down all the time. Understanding the different kinds of debt and when to get into debt is important.

  - o Debt can be classified as good debt, on-the-fence debt, mostly bad debt, and bad debt.

  - o The type of debt you take on isn't determined by whether it's a smart decision or not. Instead, it's categorized based on whether it's a good investment for your future. If the debt helps you gain financial value over time, it's a good investment. If it ends up costing you more in the long run without providing any benefits, it's not a good investment.

o Although a credit card is seen as a bad debt due to the compound interest and how easy it is to lose control, it can be beneficial if managed correctly. A credit card is a good way to build up a good credit score.

- Securing a part-time job is something every teen should consider and aspire to. Look for signs when your teen is ready to take the jump and help them create a resume. As soon as they have secured a part-time job, teach them about additional responsibilities like paying a small amount towards household expenses.

  o Safeguarding themselves and their money from emergency situations is another pivotal step in the journey. This involves insurance for the moments in life when things just don't go your way. Have a discussion with your teen about the different types of insurance and why it's important.

- Planting seeds as investments for future wealth may not be exciting to everyone at first, but the possibilities always get teens hyped up. Show them how to be responsible in investing and support them through the journey. Before you know it, they will teach you a thing or two about investing.

  o The earlier they get started, the better. Encourage them to start investing now while they don't have a lot of financial responsibilities and can take on additional risk.

  o Compound interest definitely works in their favor here, and they should take full advantage of it.

○ You may need to help them open their broker account and take responsibility for managing their investments. Have regular chats and check-ins with them to ensure that they are aware of how their investments are doing and give them the opportunity to make changes if it's needed.

○ Help them to create a diverse portfolio to limit the effect of depreciation and any sudden market changes.

● Eliminate any emotional influences that may affect their investing or spending habits.

○ Make them aware of the two concepts (emotional investing and emotional spending) and encourage them to confide in you if they ever feel like they are making emotional financial decisions.

○ Teach them the skills to identify when they are emotional, to name the emotion, and to deal with it instead of giving in to the impulse.

● Retiring rich is something we all strive for, and when you show your teen the ropes from an early age, you can ensure they reach it. No one is too young to start planning and saving for retirement. The younger they start, the more risk they can take with investments, and the higher the reward can be.

○ Setting financial goals that are specific, measurable, attainable, realistic, and time-bound will help motivate your teen to chase after and achieve them.

○ Have regular check-ins with them on the progress and make changes if their financial situation or future outlook changes.

Having all of these concepts in their toolkit will help set your teen up for success and financial freedom. Although this is a good base, encourage them to never stop learning. The more they can add to their arsenal of financial literacy, the better off they will be. We all have access to the same information, but it's the thirst for knowledge and application thereof that makes a difference.

Remember, the knowledge and skills we impart to the younger generation today will shape their financial future. Start today—you have access to all the tools to create a beautiful future for them.

Next Steps

Now that you know which topics are suitable for teaching teenagers, you may be wondering about books that can help solidify what you have taught them. I highly recommend the following resources. To find them on Amazon, scan the barcode or search the title.

Financial Literacy for Young Adults Simplified

Discover How to Manage, Save, and Invest Money to Build a Secure & Independent Future

This book is perfect for those who are just starting to learn the basics of financial literacy. It breaks down topics like budgeting, saving, and investing into simple, practical steps that they can apply. It's a great way for them to build a strong financial foundation early on.

Financial Literacy for Young Adults Amplified

Prepare for Inflation & Recession, Decide Between Buying or Renting, & Borrow Smarter

For those who are ready to take their financial knowledge to the next level, this book delves into more advanced topics like inflation and recessions, preparing for major financial decisions like buying versus renting and borrowing wisely. It's the perfect resource to help you navigate real-world financial challenges.

References

Admin. (2024, March 29). How to teach your new teen driver about auto insurance. *Alloy Insurance Partners*. https://www.alloyinsurancepartners.com/blog/how-to-teach-your-new-teen-driver-about-auto-insurance/

Allcot, D. (2021, July 8). *Should your teen save for college or invest for retirement?* GO Banking Rates. https://www.gobankingrates.com/investing/strategy/should-teen-save-college-invest-retirement/

Allec, L. (2024, June 14). *Teens and income taxes*. The Balance. https://www.thebalancemoney.com/teens-and-income-taxes-2610240

Ballinger, Dr. B. (2022, April 24). *The 6 steps to encouraging a resistant teen to get a part-time job*. Modern Parenting Solutions. https://modernparentingsolutions.org/the-6-steps-to-encouraging-a-resistant-teen-to-get-a-part-time-job/

Basic investing terms and definitions for kids & teens. (2022, March 29). Mydoh. https://www.mydoh.ca/learn/money-101/investing/basic-investing-terms-and-definitions/

Benefits of compound growth. (2024). Schwab Brokerage. https://www.schwabmoneywise.com/essentials/benefits-of-compound-growth

Boitnott, J. (2014, September 22). *40 young people who became millionaires before they were 20*. Inc.com. https://www.inc.com/john-boitnott/40-young-people-who-became-millionaires-before-they-were-20.html

Bromberg, M. (2024, April 22). *Investing for teens: What they should know*. Investopedia. https://www.investopedia.com/investing-for-teens-7111843

Buchenau, Z. (2020, February 14). *Top 10 reasons to start investing early.* Be the Budget. https://bethebudget.com/reasons-to-start-investing-early/

Budgeting 101: A guide for parents and teenagers. (2021, December 22). Mydoh. https://www.mydoh.ca/learn/money-101/money-basics/budgeting-101-a-guide-for-parents-and-teenagers/

Caballero, R. (2023, February 28). *Allow your savings to bloom: Maximize the power of compounding interest.* City Sun Times. https://www.citysuntimes.com/community_voices/allow-your-savings-to-bloom-maximize-the-power-of-compounding-interest/article_87990aa8-b71c-11ed-93be-7b50845ea042.html

Cain, S. L. (2019, June 10). 4 creative ways to pay off debt (and actually enjoy it). *Tally.* https://www.meettally.com/blog/creative-ways-to-pay-off-debt

Caldera, L. (2023a, September 12). *Best budgeting apps for teens.* Kids' Money. https://www.kidsmoney.org/teens/budgeting/apps/

Caldera, L. (2023b, September 12). *Copper banking review.* Kids' Money. https://www.kidsmoney.org/parents/money-management/copper-banking-review/

Caldera, L. (2023c, September 12). *Monarch money review.* Kids' Money. https://www.kidsmoney.org/college/money-management/monarch-review/

Children s investment education: Investment games for children: Making learning fun. (2024, June 26). FasterCapital. https://fastercapital.com/content/Children-s-Investment-Education--Investment-Games-for-Children--Making-Learning-Fun.html#

Coles, T. (2022, August 8). *Tenant insurance: A guide for parents & teens.* Mydoh. https://www.mydoh.ca/learn/money-101/insurance/tenant-insurance-a-guide-for-parents-and-teens/

Dickler, J. (2024, April 22). *83% of teenagers are already thinking about retirement — but many make this one mistake.* CNBC. https://www.

cnbc.com/2024/04/22/83percent-of-teenagers-think-about-retirement-the-best-way-to-get-started.html

Do I need to file a tax return? (2024, January 16). International Revenue Service. https://www.irs.gov/help/ita/do-i-need-to-file-a-tax-return

Dutta, B. (2022, June 30). Emotional investment: How to avoid it? *Analytics Steps.* https://analyticssteps.com/blogs/emotional-investment-how-avoid-it

EarlyBird Team. (2023, February 13). Investing for teens: How to get started. *EarlyBird.* https://www.getearlybird.io/blog/investing-for-teens

8 tips for teaching teens how to save money. (n.d.). MoneySense. https://natwest.mymoneysense.com/parents/articles/8-tips-for-teaching-teens-how-to-save-money/

Emotional investing and steps to avoid it. (2023, March 31). Guaranty Trust Fund Managers. https://www.gtfundmanagers.com/our-insights/what-is-emotional-investing/

Ethan. (2023). *SMART goals.* Khan Academy. https://www.khanacademy.org/college-careers-more/financial-literacy/xa6995ea67a8e9fdd:financial-goals/xa6995ea67a8e9fdd:smart-goals/a/smart-goals

Fay, B. (2023a, December 1). *Compound interest: How it works.* Debt.org. https://www.debt.org/advice/compound-interest-how-it-works/#

Fay, B. (2023b, December 4). *Demographics of debt.* Debt.org. https://www.debt.org/faqs/americans-in-debt/demographics/

Fernando, J. (2024a, May 31). *Dividend yield: Meaning, formula, example, and pros and cons.* Investopedia. https://www.investopedia.com/terms/d/dividendyield.asp

Fernando, J. (2024b, July 25). *Earnings per share (EPS): What it means and how to calculate it*. Investopedia. https://www.investopedia.com/terms/e/eps.asp

Fernando, J. (2024c, July 30). *Price-to-earnings (P/E) ratio: Definition, formula, and examples*. Investopedia. https://www.investopedia.com/terms/p/price-earningsratio.asp

5 fun ways to teach compound interest. (2023, January 11). Ramsey Solutions. https://www.ramseysolutions.com/financial-literacy/teaching-compound-interest

Flynn, K. (2024, January 22). *Medicare tax: What is it and who pays it?* Investopedia. https://www.investopedia.com/medicare-tax-definition-5115380

Folger, J. (2024, February 27). *Roth IRA withdrawal rules*. Investopedia. https://www.investopedia.com/roth-ira-withdrawal-rules-4769951

Geary, L. H. (2022, December 13). *Saving for retirement when you're in your 20s*. Bankrate. https://www.bankrate.com/retirement/retirement-saving-tips-for-20s/

Gleeson, L. (2022, March 23). What teens need to know about buying a car. *Mydoh*. https://www.mydoh.ca/learn/blog/lifestyle/what-teens-need-to-know-about-buying-a-car/

Gobler, E. (2022, June 30). *How to prepare your teen for their first financial investment*. The Balance. https://www.thebalancemoney.com/prepare-teen-first-investment-5203666

Good Good Piggy. (2023, September 8). *10 quotations for teaching kids money management with good good piggy*. Medium. https://goodgoodpiggy.medium.com/10-quotations-for-teaching-kids-money-management-with-good-good-piggy-bda296cc67f1

Green, N. (2024, May 28). *Compound interest: How it works in saving and investing*. Unbiased. https://www.unbiased.co.uk/discover/

personal-finance/savings-investing/compound-interest-how-it-works-in-saving-and-investing

A guide to diversification for kids, teens and parents. (2022, August 4). Greenlight. https://greenlight.com/learning-center/investing/a-guide-to-diversification-for-kids-teens-and-parents

Haverkamp, K. (2024, January 29). *The pros and cons of teen credit cards.* Refi. https://refi.com/pros-and-cons-of-teen-credit-cards/

Hazell, A. (2019). *Compound interest calculator.* The Calculator Site. https://www.thecalculatorsite.com/finance/calculators/compoundinterestcalculator.php

Helping teens use credit wisely. (n.d.). Schwab Moneywise. https://www.schwabmoneywise.com/teaching-kids/using-credit-wisely

Herrity, J. (2023, March 17). *8 budgeting methods to help you reach your financial goals.* Indeed. https://www.indeed.com/career-advice/career-development/budgeting-methods

Honda, K. (2021, April 28). *There are 7 money personality types, says psychology expert. Which one are you?* CNBC. https://www.cnbc.com/2021/04/28/7-money-personality-types-and-the-pitfalls-of-each.html

How our brains trick us into making poor investment choices. (n.d.). FasterCapital. https://fastercapital.com/topics/how-our-brains-trick-us-into-making-poor-investment-choices.html

How to avoid emotional investing. (2023, July 18). Farm Bureau Financial Services. https://www.fbfs.com/learning-center/how-to-avoid-emotional-investing

How to help your teen build good credit. (2024, June 5). Fidelity. https://www.fidelity.com/learning-center/personal-finance/teach-teens-about-credit

How to open a bank account for a minor. (n.d.). US Bank. https://www.usbank.com/bank-accounts/how-to-open-a-bank-account-for-a-minor.html

How to pay off debt fast: A guide for parents and teens. (2022, August 17). Mydoh. https://www.mydoh.ca/learn/money-101/debt/how-to-pay-off-debt-fast-a-guide-for-parents-and-teens/

How to start saving for retirement in your teens and 20s. (2023, March 3). *Slavic401k.* https://slavic401k.com/how-to-start-saving-for-retirement-in-your-teens-and-20s/

How to teach your teenager about budgeting. (2022, December 16). *Go Henry.* https://www.gohenry.com/us/blog/financial-education/how-to-teach-your-teenager-about-budgeting

Huggins, T. (2024, March 25). *How to read a pay stub.* Investopedia. https://www.investopedia.com/how-to-read-your-paycheck-5094518

Insights. (2022, August 24). *The power of compounding interest explained.* Endowus. https://endowus.com/insights/power-of-compounding-interest

Investing for kids and teens. (2023, July 27). *Great Lakes Credit Union.* https://www.glcu.org/blog/blog-details/?news_cat=money-smarts&news_article=investing-for-kids-and-teens

Jackson, M. (2022, July 8). *Money mindset: Understanding emotional spending & ways to overcome it.* Mary Rigg Neighborhood Center. https://www.maryrigg.org/money-mindset-understanding-emotional-spending-ways-to-overcome-it/

Junior Achievement. (n.d.). *Sample monthly budget.* Junior Achievement USA. https://jausa.ja.org/dA/d68a317e7b/file/JA+Teen+Budgeting+Income+and+Spending+Worksheet.pdf

KaPow Curriculums. (2023, December 18). *Your future, your choice: Why teens should care about retirement planning.* Wealthy and Rad. https://www.wealthyandrad.com/post/your-future-your-choice-why-teens-should-care-about-retirement-planning

Karr, A. (2021, December 22). *Why kids and teens should start saving money early.* Mydoh. https://www.mydoh.ca/learn/money-101/

money-basics/why-kids-and-teens-should-start-saving-money-early/

Lake, R. (2023, June 28). *Best compound interest accounts*. Forbes. https://www.forbes.com/advisor/banking/best-compound-interest-accounts/

Larson, S. (2023, August 5). *Resume examples for teens: Template and writing tips*. Indeed. https://www.indeed.com/career-advice/resumes-cover-letters/resume-examples-for-teens

Leonard, D. (2023, March 14). Job interview questions for teens and sample answers. *Mydoh*. https://www.mydoh.ca/learn/blog/career/job-interview-questions-for-teens-and-sample-answers/

Liscomb, M. (2022, September 15). *College money mistakes*. BuzzFeed. https://www.buzzfeed.com/meganeliscomb/college-money-mistakes

Liv. (2020, October 10). *15+ debt tracker ideas to help you visualize your debt-free journey*. Funding Cloud Nine. https://www.fundingcloudnine.com/debt-tracker/

Lobell, K. O. (2024, May 12). *Money foundations for kids: Compound interest*. Money Geek. https://www.moneygeek.com/financial-planning/compound-interest-for-kids/

Martucci, B. (2023, June 26). *How to calculate debt-to-income ratio for a mortgage or loan*. Money Crashers. https://www.moneycrashers.com/how-to-calculate-debt-to-income-ratio-mortgage-loan/

McCubbin, S. (2024, April 13). *11 good reasons teenagers should get a job (in 2024)*. 10 Minute Momentum. https://tenminutemomentum.com/8-reasons-teenagers-should-get-a-job/

McCurrach, D. (2024, July 8). *Retirement planning basics for teens*. Kids' Money. https://www.kidsmoney.org/teens/investing/retirement/

Mepham, J. (2021, July 14). *6 reasons why your teen needs a Roth IRA*. TheStreet. https://www.thestreet.com/retirement-daily/saving-investing-for-retirement/6-reasons-why-your-teen-needs-a-roth-ira

MK Staff. (2016, August 15). *Help your teen balance a job and school.* Metrokids. https://www.metrokids.com/help-your-teen-balance-a-job-and-school/

Modu, E. (2024, January 2). *7 steps to start investing as a teenager.* TeenVestor. https://www.teenvestor.com/7steps

Mollah, M. (2023, November 8). Teaching your teen about health insurance: A vital life skill. *Wellistic.* https://www.wellistic.com/blog/teaching-your-teen-about-health-insurance/

Naik, A. (2022, November 11). What is compound interest? Explaining to kids and teens. *Go Henry.* https://www.gohenry.com/us/blog/financial-education/what-is-compound-interest-explaining-to-kids-and-teens

Naik, A. (2023, November 22). How to stop your teen from impulsive spending. *Go Henry.* https://www.gohenry.com/uk/blog/financial-education/how-to-stop-your-teen-from-impulsive-spending

Pan, S. (2019, April 25). Retirement savings tips for teens: How to build a million-dollar IRA. *Pantheon Wealth Planning.* https://www.pantheonwealthplanning.com/blog/retirement-savings-tips-for-teens-how-to-build-a-million-dollar-ira

The parents guide to helping your teen get a job. (2021, October 21). *Mydoh.* https://www.mydoh.ca/learn/blog/career/parents-guide-to-helping-your-teen-get-a-job/

Paris, D. (2022, April 8). *How to teach kids & teens about insurance.* Mydoh. https://www.mydoh.ca/learn/money-101/insurance/how-to-teach-kids-teens-about-insurance/

Psychology of investing. (n.d.). EToro. https://www.etoro.com/investing/psychology-of-investing/

Qadar, S. (2019, November 10). How to recognise the difference between good and bad debt. *ABC News.* https://www.abc.net.au/news/2019-11-11/how-to-recognise-the-difference-between-good-and-bad-debt/11664212

A quote by Paul Samuelson. (n.d.). Goodreads. https://www.goodreads.com/quotes/9927449-investing-should-be-more-like-watching-paint-dry-or-watching

Rahn, A. (2022, July 12). *Simple and fun budgeting activities for high school students.* Metro Parent. https://www.metroparent.com/parenting/advice/simple-and-fun-budgeting-activities-for-high-school-students/

Rainey, W. (2021, July 24). *Avoiding the swamp: How to teach your kids about bad debt.* Blue Tree Savings. https://www.bluetreesavings.com/post/teaching-kids-about-bad-debt

Raypole, C. (2021, September 24). *Yes, you can find work as a teen with social anxiety: 10 jobs to try.* Healthline. https://www.healthline.com/health/anxiety/jobs-for-teens-with-social-anxiety

Reed, C. (2022, March 14). *50+ debt free quotes for motivation to pay off debt.* The Dollar Budget. https://thedollarbudget.com/debt-free-quotes/

Robinson, R. (2023, April 8). 112 motivational quotes to hustle harder and become a better entrepreneur this year. *RyRob.* https://www.ryrob.com/motivational-quotes/

Shah, H., & Jain, A. (2024, July 23). *Beginner's guide: 12 tips for diversifying your investments.* Forbes Advisor. https://www.forbes.com/advisor/in/investing/beginners-guide-12-tips-for-diversifying-your-investments/

Sharpe, C. (2023, September 12). *You need a budget (YNAB) review.* Kids' Money. https://www.kidsmoney.org/college/budgeting/ynab-review/

Singletary, M. (2013, April 1). Allowances and teenage jobs should have strings attached. *The New York Times.* https://www.nytimes.com/roomfordebate/2013/04/01/allowances-jobs-and-teaching-the-value-of-a-dollar/allowances-and-teenage-jobs-should-have-strings-attached

Sitar, D. (2021, September 14). *What is considered good debt vs. bad debt? – differences.* Money Crashers. https://www.moneycrashers.com/good-debt-vs-bad-debt/

Stalter, K., Curcio, P., & Tony, D. (2024, May 17). *What is the standard deduction?* CNN Underscored. https://edition.cnn.com/cnn-underscored/money/standard-deduction

Stockpile, Inc. (2022, September 22). *Parents are biggest influence on the way teens think about money.* PRWeb. https://www.prweb.com/releases/parents-are-biggest-influence-on-the-way-teens-think-about-money-832667145.html

Tan, C. (2022, May 13). *The 4 stages of emotional investing – to embrace or to avoid?* Poems. https://www.poems.com.sg/market-journal/the-4-stages-of-emotional-investing-to-embrace-or-to-avoid/

Teaching your kids to spend wisely. (2020, January 25). *AMP.* https://www.amp.com.au/insights-hub/blog/managing-money/kids-finance-education/teaching-kids-to-spend-wisely

Team Sammy. (2024, February 16). Compound interest: 10 sammyriffic quotes to share with kids! *Sammy Rabbit.* https://sammyrabbit.com/blog/compound-interest-10-sammyriffic-quotes-to-share-with-kids

Teen banking budgeting for teens. (n.d.). Copper. https://www.getcopper.com/guide/budgeting#

Tips to help you teach your teen to invest. (2022, November 13). *1Life Insurance.* https://www.1life.co.za/blog/tips-to-teach-teen-how-to-invest

Top 33 insurance quotes (better safe than sorry). (2023, December 28). Gracious Quotes. https://graciousquotes.com/insurance-quotes/

12 tips to use a credit card but not end up in debt. (n.d.). Credit Counselling Society. https://nomoredebts.org/credit/how-to-use-credit-card

Ward, S. (2023, May 31). *Why diversification is important in investing.* US News & World Report. https://money.usnews.com/investing/investing-101/articles/why-diversification-is-important-in-investing

Warren Buffett quote. (n.d.). A-Z Quotes. https://www.azquotes.com/quote/689478?ref=emotional-investment

What are the differences between 529 plans? (2021, June 23). Consumer Financial Protection Bureau. https://www.consumerfinance.gov/ask-cfpb/what-are-the-differences-between-529-plans-en-2078/

What is the difference between an HMO, EPO, and PPO? (n.d.). Cigna. https://www.cigna.com/knowledge-center/hmo-ppo-epo

What to do after a car accident: A step-by-step guide. (2022, October). Allstate. https://www.allstate.com/resources/car-insurance/in-case-of-a-car-accident

What's on a pay stub. (n.d.). In *Consumer Finance.* Consumer Financial Protection Bureau. https://files.consumerfinance.gov/f/documents/cfpb_parents_pay-stub-activity.pdf

Why teenagers should save for retirement (and how to get started). (2024, January 26). Milestone Asset Management Group. https://milestoneamg.com/2024/01/26/why-teenagers-should-save-for-retirement/

Wisner, W. (2022, February 9). *How to stop emotional spending (aka retail therapy).* Verywell Mind. https://www.verywellmind.com/how-to-stop-emotional-spending-retail-therapy-5218151

www.ingramcontent.com/pod-product-compliance
Lightning Source LLC
Chambersburg PA
CBHW071658210326
41597CB00017B/2238